POOL
of WISDOM

A Spiritual Autobiography

MARY-CLARE CARDER

Pool of Wisdom
Copyright © 2020 by Mary-Clare Carder

Tellwell Talent
www.tellwell.ca

ISBN
978-0-2288-2989-8 (Hardcover)
978-0-2288-2988-1 (Paperback)
978-0-2288-2990-4 (eBook)

DEDICATION

To my beloved nephews Jeremy and Noah –
who have helped and healed their
auntie more than they know.
May you both blossom in wisdom.

TABLE OF CONTENTS

ACKNOWLEDGEMENTS

A single person does not write a book—a community does.

Allen Callahan

There is no truer statement about this book. I wish first of all to thank my parents, who never wavered in their faith in God. My mother, Mary, in particular, first introduced me to the Christian path. Her abiding commitment to the spiritual journey remains an inspiration. It was marvellous to have her as a contemplative prayer companion for many years. I thank my father, Al, for being the deep-thinking man that he was. His authorship of four books was part of my inspiration to write this book. I thank my sister, Judith, and my brother, Andrew, for being the special, supportive people they are and for their part in a family I have always been happy and very grateful to be a member of. I am also extremely grateful to Judith for helping to financially support the publication of this book.

There are so many people and different groups I am grateful to. There are people whose names I will never know but who, by their wonderful presence and kind acts, have created a lasting impression and been a profound inspiration. Also the many people who, as Helen Keller puts it, produced "the wandering seeds that drop unperceived into my soul."[1] You cannot help but learn from amazing people. You also learn from people you find very difficult to be with—you hope you learn how not to be!

My thanks to Margot Galloway and my uncle Peter Mackarness, who sowed seeds in my formative spiritual development and woke me up regarding the nature of unseen realms. And to Les Dukes, an amazing medium I met when I was seventeen.

The spiritual mentor who has most influenced me is Cynthia Bourgeault. Since I first heard her speak in 1994, Cynthia's teaching has allowed me to deepen my spiritual journey, and you will find her quoted often in this book. I also wish to thank her for her extremely helpful corrections and suggestions in the "Centering Prayer" chapter. Others I must mention for their amazing spiritual presence and ability to transform are Jean Vanier, who delivered the most transformative sermon I have ever heard (Yes, Jean, we have much to learn from the disabled), Thomas Keating, Lynn Bauman, Bruno Barnhart, Henri Nouwen, Joyce Rupp, Thomas Merton, Desmond Tutu, and the amazing Mahatma Gandhi. From their own particular bright spots in the communion of saints, I am certain Geoff and Mary Flagg have helped with this book. I wish to thank Herbert O'Driscoll not only for his great gift of storytelling and teaching but also for his support and encouragement of this endeavour.

I give thanks especially to the congregations of St. Luke's in Beaverlodge, AB, and St. David-by-the-Sea and St. George's, both in Victoria, BC. These church families have been crucibles of the spiritual journey throughout my life and have provided amazing encounters as well as some difficult lessons. Many thanks to Elizabeth Eede for her gifts of Reiki healing and massage. Those gifts eased my physical pain and inflammation on many occasions. I thank the community at Queenswood Centre, the former home of the Sisters of St. Ann in Victoria, BC (now, sadly, closed), where I first heard Cynthia Bourgeault speak. The Sisters at Queenswood also offered me space, peace, and lovely meals so that I could spend time writing this book. As well I thank my family for providing a cozy cottage in a beautiful and peaceful setting on the west coast of Vancouver Island so I could spend many hours of quality time hammering out the early drafts of the manuscript. My thanks to the first prayer group I belonged to; many seeds were sown there. I am grateful to the Anglican Diocese of British Columbia and the Contemplative Society for bursaries to attend several retreats in the times when I could not afford them on my own. Lastly, once again, my grateful thanks to the Contemplative Society, whose retreats and quiet days have taught me many, many things, especially the preciousness of deep silence and many of the practices discussed in the "Inner Work—Inner Awareness" chapter.[2] Many members of the Contemplative Society are in a class by themselves for their wisdom and kindness. To Heather, Jessie, Jacquie, Marcia, Marjorie, and Yvonne, fellow spiritual travellers when this book was in its infancy, thank you for your wisdom. I also give grateful thanks to my fellow contemplative Brian, a man of gratitude, for his daily prayers for me.

Many, many thanks to my extremely knowledgeable and helpful editor Audrey McClellan. She was not only the editor of three of the four books my dad wrote but has also passed to a second generation by guiding this book through the process. This book is a far, far better work than it would have been without her editing skills. Through her knowledge of the book publishing world Audrey has also given me excellent advice through the publishing process as well.

Finally, my thanks to all at Tellwell Talent who saw this book through the publishing process. You did a fine job.

There are hundreds (if not thousands) who have contributed to this book without knowing it—a community indeed. It is, in fact, a communion of saints not only in this seen realm but also in the unseen realm. I am deeply grateful to all.

In the beginning and at the end, all healing and wisdom come from unseen realms. Come! Let us explore unseen realms.

INTRODUCTION

Welcome to this space—I pray it will be a blessing. I hope that this book will not only provide nourishment in difficult times but will also increase inner awareness and help us explore more fully our *inscape,* as Thomas Merton called it, with our whole heart sensing and exploring this inner landscape. The process of writing this book has helped me see the kingdom or the realm of God more clearly, and I hope the book itself will have the same effect for other seekers, bringing the realm more sharply into focus.

This book has two wellsprings. The first is a collection of ideas and writings that have moved me deeply and helped me on my journey in life. The second is my own spiritual experience. This book is in many ways a deeply personal study. Because Christianity is my chosen faith, and I am most familiar with Christian spirituality, this book focuses on the person of Jesus. However, you will also find wisdom from other major religions. As the Benedictine monk Bede Griffiths said, the five major world religions are like the fingers on a hand; if you go deep enough, they all merge.[3]

These two wellsprings form a pool of wisdom. When I think of a pool, I think of refreshing reservoirs. Pools of light and joy are important in our lives as they sustain us through our trials. Pools of water are absolutely necessary for our sustenance and growth. As to wisdom, it can be defined many ways, but

I will use writer Paulo Coelho's description: "Wisdom means both to know and to transform."[4] Thus, I hope this book will bring both knowledge and transformation. Cynthia Bourgeault has a very practical take on wisdom. She says, "The practice of attention and surrender—between those two banks wisdom flows."[5] From time to time throughout the book I will refer to these two simple but enlightening "banks."

Like life, this book is a journey—a journey into interior space. My journey to the interior life has come partly as a result of what I consider to be a challenging, frustrating, and disappointing exterior life. Despite my best efforts, my exterior life has not turned out at all the way I hoped. I failed to have good health, failed to marry, failed to have children, failed to have the career I wanted. In some ways it seems like a life that didn't happen. With all the disappointment in my exterior life, it is hardly a surprise that I have gravitated toward, and been guided to, the interior life. The interior life has not disappointed me! Therefore, I hope this book will be a blessing and a comfort to people with challenging exterior lives.

Due to a painful chronic disease, I have limited physical energy. This has led me to frequently ask how I can best use this limited energy. Again, the answer has been the inner or spiritual journey. Following in the footsteps of many who made the same discovery, I have found my interior life to be a great blessing—awesome at times. Even when my exterior life is not going the way I wanted or hoped it would, my interior life has always welcomed me home. Although the inner journey can be difficult, I have found it offers rest for the weary, and with a painful disease that never goes into remission, I am often weary. As Jesus said, "My yoke is easy, and my burden is light" (Matthew 11:30). I have no doubt that he was referring to the interior life. It could be said that when our exterior lives are squeezed, our interior journey is what comes out. (And there are those who think God got squeezed and the universe is what came out.)

To be of help and comfort to others is one reason I wrote this book, but there is another more selfish reason. I am reminded of a line in the African-American spiritual "Guide My Feet": "for I don't want to run this race in vain!" I know deep down that the race is not in vain, but I have a strong desire to tell others about my particular race.

Benedictine abbot Thomas Keating has written, "The only way you can fail at prayer is to fail to show up." The interior life is similar. We think we have to work hard at our spiritual lives, but usually all we have to do is show up. The yoke is easier and the burden lighter than we can imagine.

I found this book a challenge to organize, mainly, I think, because everything is related to everything else. As well, I am not a theologian, and there are *many* holes in my knowledge. There are enough holes that perhaps this book should have been called "Net of Wisdom"! "Through a glass darkly" (1 Corinthians 13:12) is an apt description of my understanding and my attempt to articulate it. Like all journeys (and, for that matter, like the universe), my inner life and my knowledge are continuously evolving.

I have tried to provide examples that show how inner inspirations can give rise to and affect the outer world. As you read the stories in this book, I hope you will be reminded of your own stories in spiritual space and will reflect and meditate on them. If this happens, the book will have fulfilled one of my hopes for it.

I also provide an overview of spiritual practices here, without going into detail about the finer points. If you wish further direction, consult the list in "Books for Further Reading and Reflection," where I've named some books I've found particularly helpful.

Some readers will find that they have encountered much of the material in this book before; to others, much will be new, challenging, and even disturbing. If at times you feel as though you have been thrown into the deep end of the pool, don't panic. This might be a good thing. I believe that all living beings swim naturally in the deep waters of the interior realm. We know this deep knowledge in our hearts, but we need to be reminded of it and discover it again.

Whatever your situation, I pray that this book will be a *pool of wisdom* for you, deep, refreshing, nourishing, and healing. Plunge in! It is my joy to share.

THE INNER UNIVERSE

The Way lies inward, to the Light hidden deep in
the heart of man.

Helen Greaves, The Wheel of Eternity

The further up and the further in you go, the bigger
everything gets. The inside is larger than the outside.

Mr. Tumnus, the faun, in The Last Battle from
"The Chronicles of Narnia" by C.S. Lewis

Conscience is the door—the sole legitimate and
healthy one—to a world at least as vast, and much
more profound, than the world that we perceive
with the senses.

Valentin Tomberg, Meditations on the Tarot[6]

Life is an *amazing* gift, and the outer world can be an indescribably beautiful and marvellous place. I am simply awestruck by the profound and vast beauty of the universe, the great variety and magnificence of nature, and I revel in humanity's constant relationship with other organisms.

However, the exterior world is a harsh place as well; it can be a world of consume or be consumed, where unfairness and evil prevail. Perhaps we can be helped to understand the harshness of the world by the following statements. Theologian and scientist John Polkinghorne has an interesting take on suffering and evil in creation: "That there is cancer in creation is not something that a more competent or compassionate Creator could easily have eliminated, but is the necessary cost of a creation allowed to make itself."[7] I am also taken with Annie Dillard's line about creation: "Creation itself was the fall, a burst into the thorny beauty of the real."[8]

It seems that in the reality of creation we cannot have beauty without the thorny. In the Serengeti I witnessed a lioness killing a beautiful little Thomson's gazelle. It was disturbing to watch, and a disaster for the gazelle, but in the larger picture, for the ecosystem, it was necessary for the lions' sustenance. When we look at the larger picture of the whole, of other realms, the harshness in life becomes transfigured.

In this exterior world there is a horrendous amount going on, and our senses are constantly bombarded. Is it any wonder that most of us spend so much of our lives concerned with the outer world? Yet if we stay in the world of our outer senses, sooner or later we become bored, sickened, or unhappy even to the point of suicide; some develop addictions to dull the pain. If we have any inner sense at all, we understand these experiences are a call to inner, deeper realms.

Much is made of our physical and intellectual health in this exterior world. We hear over and over that physical exercise for our bodies and intellectual exercise for our brains will help to keep us healthy and slow the aging process. This is good and necessary, but why is there rarely any mention of our spiritual health? Sadly, it is ignored and pushed aside. We forget that "We are spiritual beings having a human experience." If only our spiritual health was emphasized as much and even put first. How different life would be. I have no doubt that the world would be a more loving and beautiful place. As one example, I believe there would be far fewer people with addictions and mental illnesses.

"Seek first the kingdom of God," Jesus told his disciples, "and the rest will follow" (Luke 12:31).

Jesus . . . that amazing person! It seems anything could happen and did happen in his presence. For Christians, Jesus is the master of great depths and the inner journey. He constantly talks about and manifests the nearness of the kingdom of God. When he speaks of the kingdom of God or the kingdom of heaven, he seems to be speaking of the innermost being, the realm of the heart. "The kingdom of God is within you [or amongst you]," he said (Luke 17:21).

What does it mean to seek the kingdom of God? To me it means the journey or work of the heart. The kingdom of God and the heart are inseparable. As Nietzsche said, in *A Heart Full of Contradictions,* "The kingdom of God . . . is something experienced in the heart; it is everywhere and nowhere." Even so, we must actively seek it, not simply be open to it (although the latter is a good step in the right direction).

As I have gone on the inward journey, I have found that the heart is an immense place—perhaps the only truly infinite place we know. Physically it is nothing and yet . . . it holds everything. Makarios the Great, an early Christian mystic, understood this and described it beautifully:

> The heart itself is only a small vessel,
> yet dragons are there, and lions,
> there are poisonous beasts, and all the
> treasures of evil,
> there are rough and uneven roads,
> there are precipices;
> but there too is God and the angels,
> life is there, and the Kingdom,
> there too is light, and there the apostles
> and heavenly cities,
> and treasures of grace.
> All things lie within that little space.

A more recent description of the heart, the best one that has been brought to my attention, is found in Kabir Edmund Helminski's excellent book *Living Presence*.

> We have subtle subconscious faculties we are not using. Beyond the limited analytical intellect is a vast realm of mind that includes psychic and extrasensory abilities; intuition; wisdom; a sense of unity; aesthetic, qualitative, and creative faculties; and image-forming and symbolic capacities. Though these faculties are many, we give them a single name with some justification, because they are operating best when they are in concert. They comprise a mind, moreover, in spontaneous connection to the Cosmic Mind. This total mind we call "heart."[9]

It seems almost impossible to put into words all the meanings of "heart," but this description is excellent, in my opinion. The heart is indeed a vast place and a mysterious one, and it does operate best when the faculties are working in concert. As to where the heart is found, Henri Nouwen uses the image of the hub of a wheel to talk about the heart. He says, "When I move along the rim [of the wheel], I can reach one spoke after another but when I stay at the hub, I am in touch with all the spokes at once."[10] At the centre, everything works in concert.

There is a line in the following prayer of St. Patrick, "Your image deep within us." St. Patrick nestles this line right in the middle of our lives. This is no accident.

> Bless to us, O God,
> The morning sun that is above us,
> The good earth that is beneath us,
> The friends that are around us,
> Your image deep within us,
> The day which is before us.

In the middle of our lives there is an innate yearning to seek out this image of God "deep within us." Yet there is so much activity and so many distractions in our lives that, inevitably, we are reluctant to go on this inner exploration, and we may even resist the journey. I have had experience of this.

A wonderful Sufi story explains our reluctance to pursue inner or spiritual work.[11] A person is looking in his garden for a key that he has lost. People come to help him in his search. They look all around the garden for some time until finally someone asks him, "Well, where did you lose it?" The person replies, "I lost it inside the house." Someone then asks, "If you lost it inside, what are you doing looking for it outside?" The person replies, "It's dark in there, and there are people to help out here, and lots of interesting things going on."

This story illustrates beautifully some important points about spiritual work. First, as stated above, the key is inside.[12] This echoes Jesus's words: "The kingdom of God is within you." Second, the exterior world is often a fun and interesting place—certainly it seems more fun and interesting than the spiritual journey, which I have found may be dark and lonely, and not easy. A retired clergy friend, Derek, has a wonderful description of the never-ending work of spiritual growth and transformation. He says, "I'm waiting for the other shoe to drop, and I feel like a centipede."

In fact, however, the physical/outer world is not separated from the inner world. Everything works as a whole. Kabbalah says, "As above, so below." It can also be said, "As inside, so outside." In this way, the horizontal and the vertical come together, forming for Christians the symbol of the cross.

"The glory of God is a human being fully alive," said Bishop Irenaeus in the third century.[13] In other words, the evolutionary destiny for humanity on this planet is a fully developed consciousness, awareness, or heart. Christians would call this "the Christ consciousness"; another name for it would be "cosmic consciousness." The development of consciousness comes from inner work, whose fruit is spiritual transformation and its outer manifestations.

I believe the most tragic thing in this life is to refuse to go on the spiritual/religious journey. If we refuse, we miss out on the most wonderful party (or banquet, as Jesus calls it) the cosmos has to offer. We are *always* being called to the banquet. Alleluia!

> Only with awakened hearts are we actually able to fulfill our purpose within the cosmos and take our place in that great dance of divine manifestation.
>
> Cynthia Bourgeault, *Wisdom Way of Knowing*

The dance at the great banquet—bring it on!

SUFFERING AND INNER TRANSFORMATION

And I saw the river over which every soul must pass to reach the kingdom of heaven and the name of that river was suffering: and I saw a boat which carries souls across the river and the name of that boat was love.

St. John of the Cross

There is no coming to consciousness without pain.

Carl Jung

I have learned that even when I have pains, I don't have to be one!

Maya Angelou

It seems we are destined to experience the dance and the banquet as well as the river of suffering. But why must we suffer? This is the unanswerable question everyone has.

I once heard an American Protestant clergyman say, "God is not all powerful because love limits power." Is this why there is suffering—and evil—in the world? Perhaps the goal of our journey of inner transformation is to be able to hold both the boat and the river in our hearts so that we experience love as well as suffering. This is a mystical paradox of this world.

Is it as William Blake says, "And we are put on this earth a little space that we might learn to bear the beams of love"? When I was young and someone did something very kind for me, I would get embarrassed and hardly be able to stand it. However, as I have temporally and spiritually matured I feel far less embarrassment. I hope it is because I am learning to bear the beams of love a little better.

The main characters in Rohinton Mistry's novel *A Fine Balance* live destitute and hopeless lives and face every adversity imaginable in the slums of India. Yet the author writes with enough compassion, and sometimes humour, that the reader can bear to read about their terrible suffering. Many of us know what suffering is like if compassion isn't present. That road is very dark indeed, and we experience hell on Earth.

As in *A Fine Balance,* it is much easier to endure the river of suffering in our own lives if we can be borne in a boat of love. Although that boat often seems fragile and leaky, we can strengthen it through inner or spiritual work.

There is one positive side to suffering that I can think of: those who suffer are more interested in transforming the world. If everything is going along swimmingly, you want to float on the surface of life and leave things as they are.

Ultimately, perhaps the vision of St. John of the Cross, quoted above, alludes to the idea that joy and suffering are aspects of the same phenomenon—as well expressed by the novelist Julien Green: "When you think of the mystical experience of many saints, you may ask yourself whether joy and suffering aren't aspects of the same phenomenon on a very high level. An analogy, crazy for sure, comes to my mind: extreme cold burns. It seems nearly certain, no, it is certain, that we can only go to God through suffering and that this suffering becomes joy because it finally is the same thing."[14] In my gut I am sure the statement by Green is correct, but in difficult moments I am not at that resolution yet.

This idea is very Hegelian: "Once the two opposites in anything had resolved their conflict, they would synthesize, and the thing they were would cease to be. Thus all life was only a becoming, never a being. And all of creation was simply pieces and parts of some great Absolute that was itself becoming."[15] My intuition tells me that this statement has truth too.

Franciscan priest Richard Rohr says that there are two ways to inner transformation: suffering and prayer. In the end, he suggests that there is only one way to inner transformation and that is through suffering, since we usually come to prayer through suffering. Leonard Cohen has written an excellent description of how transformation often works:

> Ring the bells that still can ring,
> Forget your perfect offering.
> There is a crack in everything.
> That's how the light gets in.

We can get so stuck and rigid, looking at something a certain way, that no further movement can happen unless we crack. That is how the light gets in and transformation comes into being. I have certainly seen that happen in my life. For example, when I have seen someone do something so compassionate it breaks me open (I even feel badly for not having the thought and the courage to have done it myself), or when I have experienced a different culture and begun to see things through the eyes of its members, again I have become broken open. Being broken open is a surrender, and as Cynthia Bourgeault says, surrender is one of two parts of wisdom.

Before we go further, it may be helpful to share a little of my story. I am a lifelong Anglican, and I consider myself a mystic. From the age of twelve or thirteen I have had what I call "spiritual or mystical experiences." They have usually been a voice (not my own) inside my head. In spiritism (or spiritualism) this is called clairaudience. Sometimes I have had a sense of things that were not from this plane of existence.

The first time I remember having an experience of clairaudience, I was about twelve years old. It is a little embarrassing. I was outside, playing on our sundeck. There was an ant nest somewhere nearby, and many ants were crawling over the deck. With nothing better to do, I mindlessly—and heartlessly—began to step on the ants and kill as many of them as I could. Suddenly I heard someone say, "Stop it!" There was no one around; the voice was in my head, but it was not my own voice. I was so startled I did stop, and I never trod on another ant. *Someone* knew what I was doing.

As I mentioned in the "Introduction," I almost certainly would not have taken the spiritual journey I did without the suffering and disappointment I have faced in my life. I struggled all through my teen years from agoraphobia, which I later understood was a manifestation of post-traumatic stress disorder (PTSD) caused by a bad concussion I received when I was about eight years old. We now know people who suffer concussions can experience sensory overload from regular amounts of light and sound. It is no wonder that I had trouble processing busy, noisy places, and hence the agoraphobia. Unfortunately, little was known about the effects of concussions in the 1960s, so mine was not treated in any way.

When I was about fourteen or fifteen, I remember one time I was in tears about the agoraphobia, which would not resolve. While asking God for help, I suddenly felt an upwelling of joy. In traditional Christian language, this is the work of the Holy Spirit. The mystics called such experiences "spiritual consolations," while Cynthia Bourgeault refers to them as "vertical downloading." I had several of these experiences in my early to mid-teens. In my late teens and early twenties they seemed to dry up, but, fortunately, they have shown up again from time to time in my later life. They are an enormous blessing.

For a few short years after my teens I began to heal, cope, and manage reasonably well with the challenging agoraphobia and other after-effects of the concussion. Later, when I had a contemplative prayer (meditation) practice, one of the concepts that helped me with agoraphobia was the idea that "if you are comfortable in the desert, you will be comfortable in the marketplace." For me, practising contemplative or centering prayer is like going into the desert, where everything is stripped away. There are no props, nothing you can hide behind. If you can stand in the desert, then you can stand naked in the marketplace, so to speak. If I had known about meditation or centering prayer when I was a teenager, I may have suffered from the PTSD of the concussion, particularly the agoraphobia, for a shorter length of time.

Around 1988, at the age of twenty-nine, I began a gruelling round of suffering when I was diagnosed with Sjogren syndrome. This syndrome, named after a Swedish ophthalmologist, is an autoimmune disease with symptoms similar to rheumatoid arthritis or lupus. It is the second-most-common autoimmune disease after rheumatoid arthritis. Up to 1 percent of the population is afflicted with this syndrome, and nine out of ten are women. Even as a child I noticed I didn't have the stamina of other children. Off and on for years I had experienced times when I was unusually tired and not feeling quite right. After several months of recurring sinus infections, I was referred to an ear, nose, and throat specialist, who suspected Sjogren's. By this time, full-blown Sjogren syndrome, with accompanying arthritis, had set in.

My symptoms became progressively worse. My dry eyes, dry mouth, and arthritis were a misery. Although I tried to be optimistic, there seemed to be less and less sunshine in my life. I felt as though I was continuously swimming through a viscous pool of molasses, working hard but getting nowhere. Fatigue and pain made full-time work impossible and part-time work a struggle. I was facing a life of pain and poverty.[16] Unlike some of the autoimmune diseases, Sjogren's rarely goes into remission. I have read that there is a 1 percent chance of remission. My rheumatologist tried many of the standard treatments on me, but they didn't help much and often had damaging side effects. In fact, one medication began to damage my bone marrow. If I hadn't stopped taking it, the medication would eventually have killed me.

The pain and inflammation of the disease got to the point where I sometimes felt as though every cell in my body was screaming. At the worst times my body felt like a bag of pus. About 1995 I came to a place where I could not take it any longer. For several months I prayed that God would either let me die or make me well. I didn't care which.

During this dark period I went on a two-day silent retreat. In a one-on-one session, the retreat leader suggested I do a visualization exercise. When he asked what was bothering me the most, I told him it was my frustration. He asked me to visualize my frustration and then see what happened when Jesus entered the scene. Immediately I imagined that my frustration was represented by two large rusty cogs, their teeth grinding and straining, hardly able to move. When Jesus entered the scene, he did not bring an oil can. Instead, something very beautiful happened. Vines and flowers began to grow up and cover the cogs. I believe that this visualization opened up a totally new way of being for me. I realized I was still struggling too much, and I needed to give way to an easier, more organic way of life. Oddly enough, the theme of the retreat was the Sermon on the Mount: "Consider the lilies of the field, how they grow; they neither toil nor spin, yet I tell you, even Solomon in all his glory was not clothed like one of these" (Matthew 6:28, 29).

Shortly after this retreat I had a laying on of hands and an anointing with oil for healing at my parish church. Some family members and friends were present. It was a wonderful experience, and I know it ploughed the psychic field, so to speak—preparing me for the death of a former life and for the healing that would happen in the months to come.

On the morning of the day I went on the retreat, I was walking through my local public library and noticed a shelf of books about arthritis. I thought, "I don't think there is anything that would help me here, but I'll look anyway." I came across a book called *The Arthritis Breakthrough,* by Henry Scammell and Thomas McPherson Brown. After reading the first couple of pages, my skepticism evaporated and my mind began spinning. The authors' theory that rheumatic diseases might be caused by an allergy to a mycoplasma infection resonated with me—I had developed the first symptoms of Sjogren's around the time I had a series of sinus infections—and explained a number of things about rheumatic diseases. Scammell and Brown reported that 75 to 80 percent of the patients they had studied saw a marked improvement in their conditions after they had taken a low concentration of certain antibiotics over a long period of time. Some sufferers even went into remission after three or four years of treatment.

Taking antibiotics for a rheumatic disease was not orthodox treatment at the time, but after some consultation my G.P. allowed me to try it. I am glad she did. Early results were very promising. Within a week, after taking only 100 milligrams of minocycline, I noticed that my eyes had more moisture and my mouth more saliva than they'd had for a long time. Within ten days I was experiencing periods with very little pain for the first time in three years. I remember running and jumping along the road at that point. It was exciting.

Sadly, the pain-free periods never lasted. The minocycline treatment brought me many pools of sunlight but, disappointingly, did not put me into remission. Inflammation and pain still remained. Some other treatments have helped along the way, such as Reiki (see the chapter titled "Healing") and an antidepressant that helps me sleep and cope with the pain better.

I retain an open mind about the mycoplasma-antibiotic theory, despite the fact that a top-notch rheumatologist in Vancouver told me that the minocycline worked even when the antibiotic agent was taken out. I had always felt that the antibiotics were not confronting the disease head-on but from an angle. This would make sense if the antibiotics were addressing an aspect of the disease, which is probably the case. I now believe a cure lies in another direction.

In 2007 I happened to read a newspaper article about Dr. Michael Dosch, a researcher at Toronto's Hospital for Sick Children, who had found a possible cure for Type 1 (autoimmune) diabetes through his studies involving mice. I sent Dr. Dosch an e-mail, telling him I thought his research was very exciting for autoimmune diseases. I told him I had Sjogren syndrome and asked if he knew of any rheumatologists who were following his research in relation to other autoimmune diseases, such as Sjogren's. He replied to my e-mail, telling me that he had done research on primary Sjogren syndrome with mice and the results looked promising.

I was thrilled. To me, the most hopeful thing was the series of coincidences by which I had heard about the research. I believed it was synchronicity, "meaningful patterns of co-incidence,"[17] which seems to be the Spirit's way of tapping us on the shoulder to say, "Pay attention to this." (And remember that attention is the second part of wisdom.)

According to Dr. Dosch's research, it appears that Sjogren's sufferers produce a protein in the islet cells of the pancreas called ICA69 (ICA stands for Islet Cell Antigen), which may be the cause of the problem. Dr. Dosch developed a vaccine that blocks this protein. When this blocking vaccine was injected into mice suffering from Sjogren syndrome, the disease virtually disappeared in them.[18] If the vaccine produced the same result in humans, it could mean a cure for millions of sufferers of Sjogren's!

Unfortunately, there is a big damper on this potential breakthrough, as usual—funding. Dr. Dosch tried unsuccessfully to get funding for human trials of the vaccine. It was tantalizing to think that perhaps all that was preventing a cure (or a far superior treatment) was $250,000. Unfortunately, due in part to illness and age, Dr. Dosch gave up looking for funding for the research.

During the last few years I have searched for donors who might give $250,000, to no avail.[19] It is disheartening and frustrating when most of your e-mails, letters, and phone calls go unanswered. I am no stranger to frustration, but trying to help get the human trials up and running is perhaps the most discouraging thing I have ever been a part of. A good deal of the frustration comes from the knowledge that there are billionaires and multimillionaires out there who would not miss $250,000 in the least. I believe governments also need to step up their research funding. If medical research had been better funded in Canada in 2002, when the research with the mice was done, we might be much farther ahead in finding a cure. Pharmaceutical companies don't seem to help much either. They are more interested in making better pills than finding cures.

At times I have been disappointed to the point of being angry. When I am most frustrated I say to God, "I feel you brought this research to my attention so that I could help move it along, but all I seem to do is run into obstacles."

Despite the lack of progress, I have learned something about the process of research. Scientific research moves extremely slowly—far too slowly, in my opinion. It reminds me a little of the slow growth of our spiritual consciousness. Perhaps the two are not unrelated.

Indeed, this dark world of pain and suffering can be frightening, distressing, and depressing. In the eyes of the world, being chronically ill means you are marginalized. This is a physical world, and if you have physical weaknesses you are at a real disadvantage.

As happens for many people with debilitating illnesses, my financial situation was also precarious, and with anxiety over finances added to the pain and fatigue of Sjogren's, at times it all became too much to bear. I had to accept the fact that I would not have the career I wanted or do many of the physical things I really wanted to do. For instance, even if I could find a supportive husband whom I loved, taking care of a family would be difficult. It is hard to break out of cultural conditioning: women are expected to have both children and a successful career, and society tells us we can always do more.

Probably the cruellest thing of all about this disease is that I can look fit and healthy, even though I feel awful. Most people are understanding, but a few are not. Another difficulty is that occasionally I have had glimpses of what life would be like without Sjogren's: no pain and much more energy. The experience is wonderful at the time but disheartening and frustrating too, as I realize the possibility of a different life.

I was fortunate in my parents' loving attitude. When I was diagnosed with Sjogren's, my mother said to me, "We will always make sure you have a roof over your head, food to eat, and clothes to wear." I thank God for parents who were able and willing to help me when I needed it. I wish everyone had parents like that. Without the supportive family and interior life I have had, I would not be here to tell the tale.

I was also fortunate in my line of work. As a piano teacher I could choose my own hours, something I could never have done at a full-time or regular part-time job, where the hours are rigid. However, as a piano teacher I was often underemployed. As for disability benefits, I think the disabled are treated very badly in Canada and, I believe, in just about every country in the world. The disability pension should be above the poverty level, for one thing, and you should not need to be practically bedridden to be eligible. It proved impossible to get a disability pension from the provincial government. The Canada Pension Plan, to its credit, gave me as much pension as possible—but as I had not worked very long, I was not eligible for much.

With almost constant inflammation and often pain for over thirty years, sometimes I can't believe I am still here. Many times when I've gone through a bad patch, I wish I were dead. I have often thought, "Oh, to be out of this body, free of pain, and to have energy! Why can't anyone help me and millions of others like me? If only our spiritual consciousness were greater, we would know how to cure this disease." In light of such thoughts, a thirst for the inner life becomes unquenchable.

I used to dislike the old adage "God doesn't give us anything more than we can bear," but I think there is some truth in it. At first I found myself clinging to God for dear life, but when I was able to let go, even a bit, I began my inner journey. Just as I must visit my doctor to ask questions and seek treatment to ensure my physical health, I've found I have to keep asking, seeking, and knocking on interior and exterior doors for my spiritual journey.

It takes years (or forever) to adjust after you have been diagnosed with a debilitating, chronic disease. But one must adjust internally or you end up being crushed. As I mentioned, after you've had a chronic disease for a while, you feel yourself shifted from the mainstream to the fringes of society—and of life, to a lesser extent. If you are like me, you do not like being on the fringes of life at all; you want to *do* something and *be* someone. However, fringes—or "thin spaces," as they are called in Celtic spirituality—are often places where the

Kingdom of God is most powerfully at work. You begin to see and experience things differently.

I would strongly urge anyone suffering a debilitating disease to explore the interior life. As I wrote in the "Introduction," no matter how badly things are going in your exterior life, you will not be disappointed or discouraged in your interior life if you keep seeking it. At times it will be the only thing that gets you through the darkness and misery. No wonder Jesus said, "Seek first the kingdom of God."

In one of my times of despair and anxiety about my financial situation, I called to God in my thoughts, "Please take care of me." I heard the kindest, gentlest voice inside me say, "I will always take care of you." I would like to be able to say that my first reaction to that voice was joy and gratitude, but that was not what happened. I said, "Do you think you could do a better job? I'm having a tough time here." In hindsight, though, I am so grateful for this communication because, over and over again, it has given me hope and courage and makes me realize that even when I don't feel like I'm being taken care of, I am.

I have had a sense for several years that before I came to earth I was asked if I wanted to take on this life. I obviously, and I sense reluctantly, said yes. It is a mystery I will probably not know the truth of until I go back to the eternal.

In the worst times I have simply wanted to be out of my body and in a place where I would never again suffer physical pain. I have said to God, "I want to die." The response has been, "Your death can be arranged, but you have to make sure you have done everything you came to do here." My reply has always been (so far), "No, I haven't done everything that I came to do," and so I go on.

Of course, we cannot go on without hope. There have been moments when it takes a great deal of faith to believe that no matter what we suffer, we, like all things in creation, are cradled in the loving arms of God. I hope I am not tempting fate here, but I believe that, on the whole, the Sjogren's symptoms are marginally better than they used to be. Thanks be to God! Also, age has helped me come to terms with the reality that I will not be able to do many of the things I wanted to accomplish. They no longer have the importance they once did. What a relief!

To those who believe that suffering is an illusion or of our own making, I must disagree 100 percent. Suffering is real, and real suffering is often not of our own making. I have found myself thinking such things as "If I were a different kind of person I wouldn't have gotten sick." This may be true, but then I would not be me. We must try not to blame ourselves or let anyone else blame us for the disease. For one thing, blame puts us into egoic consciousness (ordinary consciousness—there is more about egoic consciousness in the "Inner Work—Inner Awareness" chapter), so blame and guilt hinder healing. Jesus, who in my opinion was one of the greatest healers to have graced the world, never blamed people for their disease. When his disciples asked him who was to blame for the blindness of the man in John 9, Jesus focused on "seeing the glory of God" (John 9:3) in the healing rather than assigning guilt or blame.

I have found it helps to see suffering in the widest context possible. In fact, I find this the only way I can make any sense of this kind of suffering. If I look at my suffering moment to moment, or day to day, there have been times when it seemed unbearable and pointless. If, however, I am able to look at illness on the large scale, I am very grateful to those who suffered, and often died, from such diseases as smallpox or polio. I am so sorry that millions have died from those horrendous diseases, but because of their suffering I was born into a world where polio and smallpox were virtually unheard of—two terrible diseases that I was free from and didn't have to worry about. I am sure that, in the future, people will not have to endure autoimmune diseases, such as Sjogren syndrome, because I and others suffered from them today, and eventually a cure will come to light. This brings comfort and tenderness to the heart.

A similarly wide view of suffering is held by Teilhard de Chardin, who says that "The world is still building," even though it can be painful. As Valentin Tomberg puts it, "The illusions dissipate, but at what price?" And John Polkinghorne, in a comment I quoted earlier, noted that pain and suffering "is the necessary cost of a creation allowed to make itself."

When I was first diagnosed with Sjogren syndrome, a friend who suffered from MS suggested that I read the Book of Job. You, too, may find this helpful in your journey. I have found the following meditation beneficial, and I hope others who suffer chronic pain will also feel it is useful. It is from *Praying Our Goodbyes* by Joyce Rupp.[20]

PRAYER OF ONE WHO IS IN CONSTANT
PHYSICAL PAIN.

Image: your hand touching the hem of the robe of
Jesus

Begin your prayer time by reflecting on your illness;
be aware of your feelings, both of body and of spirit.

OPENING PRAYER
God of oneness, wholeness, I hurt and pain and I dream of the day when I no longer feel continual distress in my body. I cry out to you to hear me, to stretch your arms of compassion to me and to embrace me with your comfort. My being needs to be filled with your spiritual energy. I am weary with the struggle to feel well and be in good health. It is so easy to slide into depression and self-pity, to be impatient and despondent. God of the living, hear me. Fill my empty places with hope. Fill my life with a sense of joy in spite of this ceaseless

pain. Help me to fight that giant oppressor of the spirit: discouragement. Remind me often of the good people of my life and of all the blessings that are mine as I struggle with this pain which is ever present to me. I praise and thank you for being a God who never leaves me.

REFLECTION

Read Luke 8:40-48, the story of the woman who had been ill for twelve years.

Picture yourself in the crowd. See Jesus there. See what a loving, kind person he is. Feel a drawing to him in your heart. Image yourself going to Jesus, leaning down, touching the hem of his garment. Feel the tremendous spiritual power that moves from Jesus into your whole body and soul. Hear Jesus ask: "Who touched me?" See yourself stand up and speak to Jesus. Speak whatever comes to your mind and heart. Then listen to what Jesus speaks to you. Perhaps he will tell you that you are being healed or that your pain can be a source of inner transformation, or maybe Jesus will tell you how you are to live with your pain. Perhaps he will speak no words to you at all, only look on you with a deep compassion and understanding.

Pray your response to Jesus.

CLOSING PRAYER (Psalm 18—adapted)

I love you, God. I know you are my inner strength, especially now when my body does not have the strength that I took for granted in the past. God, my deliverer, I turn to you. Sometimes I feel I do not want to go on. I get swallowed up by the floods of self-pity and discouragement. In my distress I cry out to you. Reach out to me and rescue me from the enemy of pain. Set me free of its grasp of resentment. Fill me with courage. When the darkness of constant pain threatens to overcome me, brighten the darkness with your presence. With you by my side I can go through this. You are like a rock. You will be my strength. You are like a shield. You can protect my spirit from being broken by my body's pain. I will keep coming to you, touching the hem of your garment of love and feeling the spiritual energy which you share with me. I love you and I place my trust in you. Amen.

The phrase which stays with me the most is, "I dream of the day when I no longer feel continual distress in my body." Oh how I dream of that day!

To get back to the question at the beginning of the chapter, "Why is there suffering and evil in the world?" Maybe we will learn that love is stronger than suffering and evil. Despite suffering and evil, in our inmost being we can still be bathed in the light of love. (We will learn more about being in the presence of love in "The Unrecognized Gift of Silence" and "Centering Prayer.") Perhaps one reason for my own difficulties in this realm is that I am to bear witness and help the world break free of the sufferings which have so afflicted my own life.

THE UNFOLDING OF
CONSCIOUSNESS

I regard consciousness as fundamental. I regard
matter as derivative from consciousness. We cannot
get behind consciousness.

Max Planck[21]

In the previous chapter I referred a couple of times to the
slow growth of our spiritual consciousness. During our
short existence in this universe we learn that everything
progresses. The human consciousness is no exception to
progression or evolution. We see the evidence of this evolution
and unfolding in our own lives, and if we reflect carefully we
can see this unfolding globally as well as personally. Just as
the universe seems to be expanding faster, so too does human
consciousness. In my opinion, human consciousness could grow
much faster if we gave more attention to our spiritual growth.

Ken Wilber has built on an expanded system of the levels of
human consciousness, originally developed by Erich Neumann
a student of Carl Jung and Jean Gebser.[22] In Wilber's book
Integral Spirituality, inspired by the chakra system of Hindu
and Buddhist spirituality, Wilber uses the colour spectrum to
mark what he calls the "altitude" of conscious development.
This spectrum ranges from infrared through magenta with
the colours of the rainbow, all the way to ultraviolet and clear
light.

Magenta represents the earliest forms of human consciousness, a world of magic and animism, of clans, huts, rage, lust, rocks, rivers, trees, spearheads.

When consciousness unfolds in red, we encounter a consciousness that is egocentric, self-referential, and instinctual, a world of magic-mythic, warlords, tribes, domination, oppression, slavery, genocide, and elemental gods and goddesses.

At the amber stage the world is ethnocentric, authoritarian, and traditional, with cathedrals, righteous man, chivalry, salvation, charity, and the omnipotent, omniscient, omnipresent Great Other.

Orange represents a consciousness that is rational, pragmatic, individualistic, world-centric, and modern. This is a world of electrons, protons, a periodic table of more than 100 elements, skyscrapers, rockets, compassion, universal moral ideals, television, radio, automobiles, airplanes, and a spirit seen as the Great Designer and/or the Ground of All Being.

Green represents the postmodern world, with pluralistic systems, multiculturalism, the Internet and the World Wide Web, spirit as deep ecology, and human harmony.

Turquoise represents the global mind, the Gaian collective, differential-integral calculus, nth-dimensional hyperspace, potential energy sources, and spirit as planetary holarchy.

Indigo is the trans-global, illumined mind. There is luminous clarity and compassion, trans-planetary social ideals, mega-tribes, truth/goodness/beauty self-seen in global gestalts, and spirit as infinite light/love.

Violet represents the meta-mind and brilliant clarity of the over-mind. There is infinite love and compassion for all sentient beings from their perspective, and trans-dimensional social ideals, spirit as radical interiority, and infinite holarchy.

In Christian spirituality, I think the highest altitudes would be known as the Omega point.[23]

It is difficult to understand the later altitudes because we aren't there yet. But even if we can't fully grasp the later stages, they sound exciting!

I can look back at my life and see various stages I was at. Even more clearly, I believe I can look at world history and see how countries and the world in general are moving along the spectrum. We can't say any of those stages are right or wrong, as they all must be passed through, and various elements of ALL levels are carried forward.[24] I still sometimes love to immerse myself in the world of wizards, dragons, rivers, trees, and rocks. At the same time, I love the description of spirit as "radical interiority" at the violet stage.

We see these levels not only in physical ways—for example, in fortress castles from the amber level—but also in psychological ways. For example, going to war for ethnocentric reasons is characteristic of the amber level. By the time we get to the green and teal/post-modern levels, we become reluctant to go to war; at the turquoise/global-mind level, society doesn't go to war because it serves no purpose. At the indigo level, I imagine we embrace our enemies in non-dual love.

Coming to understand this spectrum of levels of consciousness has been enlightening for me. I find being able to see a larger picture of where we are, where we have been, and where we will go, helpful and hopeful. Our ability to view the larger picture, have a greater acceptance of mystical experiences, and use the whole of our hearts (in the Kabir Helminski sense) spurs us to higher levels.

Moving into a new level of consciousness is often not easy. A novel written over 130 years ago shows why these changes can be so hard to achieve and accept—not so much because people are against change or progress of consciousness, but because this change requires a complete shift in being, and this is difficult, especially when we are not used to working from the inside of ourselves. If you've believed one thing all your life, it can be hard to accept that there may be a different way to look at that thing. This was what Edwin A. Abbott was describing in *Flatland: A Romance of Many Dimensions*, published in 1884. The novel was written to explain a world of many dimensions, but it is also an excellent analogy of spiritual growth and the evolution of consciousness. *Flatland,* in essence, is the story of a two-dimensional square that comes to experience a three-dimensional world.

> The square describes his world as a plane populated by lines, circles, squares, triangles, and pentagons. Being two-dimensional, the inhabitants of Flatland appear as lines to one another. They discern one another's shape both by touching and by seeing how the lines appear to change in length as the inhabitants move around one another.
>
> One day, a sphere appears before the square. To the square, which can see only a slice of the sphere, the shape before him is that of a two-dimensional circle. The sphere has visited the square intent on making the square understand the three-dimensional world that he, the sphere, belongs to. He explains the notions of "above" and "below," which the square confuses with "forward" and "back." When the sphere passes through the plane of Flatland to show how he can move in three dimensions, the square sees only that the line he'd been observing gets shorter and shorter and then disappears. No matter what the sphere says or does, the square cannot comprehend a space other than the two-dimensional world that he knows.
>
> Only after the sphere pulls the square out of his two-dimensional world and into the world of Spaceland does he finally understand the concept of three dimensions. From this new perspective, the square has a bird's-eye view of Flatland and is able

to see the shapes of his fellow inhabitants (including, for the first time, their *insides*).

Armed with his new understanding, the square conceives the possibility of a fourth dimension. He even goes so far as to suggest that there may be no limit to the number of spatial dimensions. In trying to convince the sphere of this possibility, the square uses the same logic that the sphere used to argue the existence of three dimensions. The sphere, now the shortsighted one of the two, cannot comprehend this and does not accept the square's arguments— just as most of us "spheres" today do not accept the idea of extra dimensions.[25]

Like the square, we have to be able to shift our consciousness, shift from one level to the next, or undergo what is called a "paradigm change," if we want to have a happier, healthier world. The pattern for a paradigm shift is: paradigm→ chaos→ crisis→ shift→ new paradigm.[26] A certain paradigm is only relatively stable when it fits the consciousness of a society; as social consciousness shifts, things become more and more chaotic until a crisis results, at which point a new paradigm is born. With a new paradigm we find ourselves, like the square in Flatland, with an ability to see things in a totally new way and hence able to do things in ways we had not been able to conceive before.

How does this ability to come into a new paradigm happen? It is a mystery. Consciousness evolves in many ways, but if we trust in the unseen realms of God/love, we will not get stuck in Flatland.

Our ability to transition to other paradigms depends on being raised in being and working at depth, as I will discuss in the next chapter. From there, I will go on to discuss methods and practices that I believe help accelerate this growth of human consciousness and spiritual enlightenment.

INNER WORK—INNER AWARENESS:
BECOMING AN EXPRESSION
OF DIVINE LOVE

What the next revolution requires is that we work from the inside out.

Utne magazine, January–February 2006

Your vision will become clear only when you can look into your own heart. Who looks outside, dreams; who looks inside, awakes.

Carl Jung

O ur outer work is only as good as our inner work. Think of some good deed you did. I believe that the greatest part of it was the spiritual or inner work that went on inside you before the outer deed transpired. Everything begins on the inside, at depth, from an eternal realm. To have done that good outer deed, or to transform to the next level of consciousness, we must be in synchronization with the inmost part of us.

When people ask me "What is inner work?" I'm usually speechless for a little while. Like the centipede, I am waiting for the other shoe to drop. What little I know of inner work is difficult to describe or explain because it is spiritual experiential knowledge or, to use the Greek term, *gnosis*. Gnosis allows us to be more aware on the inside and, thus, more aware of other realms. As Thomas Keating puts it, inner work will stop us from running a train around and around a very small track (i.e., our ego) and set us to work on the cosmic railway. The absolute importance of inner or spiritual work is stressed for Christians in the story of Christ going out into the wilderness, after he was baptised but before he began his public work, to struggle with and transfigure his inner demons (Matthew 4:1-11, Luke 4:1-13). Struggling with, and transfiguration of, our inner demons is inner work.

Cynthia Bourgeault says, "Inner work is not a self-improvement project. It is not about improving or changing the personality." It is something more profound. It's a total transformation of consciousness and being.

For me, inner work is about two things: being raised in being, and working at depth. For Christians, the ideas of "raised" and "depth" can be seen in the vertical plane of the cross. Movement on this vertical plane is consciousness itself. Maurice Nicholl wrote: "As your Being increases [or is raised], your receptivity to higher meaning increases. As your Being decreases, the old meanings return."[27] This statement is reminiscent of Ken Wilber's altitudes and the story of Flatland. Many times I have noticed when I have been around people with lower negative energy; if I don't pay attention I can get dragged down to their level and become equally negative. Similarly when I am around an enlightened person it becomes easy for the best of my being to shine forth.

Likewise, for depth, Valentin Tomberg states, "The aim of spiritual exercises is *depth*. It is necessary to become deep in order to be able to attain experience and knowledge of profound things."[28] These statements are pivotal to understanding inner work. Jacob's ladder (Genesis 28:10-17) is an early example passed down to us of this movement. The ladder is thought to represent the perpetual dialogue between heaven and earth.

How do we become raised in being? How do we work at depth? Probably the most effective method has been practised by contemplative monks and nuns for nearly two millennia. Whether they are washing dishes, worshiping, or working on an artistic project, they are mindful of the presence of God. Being in the presence of God is continual prayer. In a word, awareness—or in two words, becoming awake!

Using certain spiritual practices (or praxis as some call it) helps us with this work of becoming awake and helps move us along the path. I have found many of the following practices, which I learned at the Contemplative Society wisdom schools, very useful:

- spending time in silence
- centering/contemplative prayer/meditation
- using the inner observer
- *lectio divina*
- chanting
- walking meditation
- full body praying
- practising presence and mindfulness

These can be done in a group or individually. On the surface they may seem geared for individual development, but at a profound level they serve humanity, the world, and the universe as a whole. When these practices are done in a group, the energy can become even more profound.

When we work at this deep, or big picture, level, I call it doing "deep background work," which, as well as I can explain it, is praying or focusing energy in a deep loving way toward the transformation of the world. Srimata Sudha Puri, a Hindu teacher and mystic, explains the impact this can have on the widest community (the universe) when she says, "When you do real spiritual work, the effect ripples out over the whole universe, whether people know it or not."[29]

Using such practices as those mentioned above, we learn about surrender, detachment, developing the inner observer, healing and transcending the ego (and with it, healing memories), and emptying the self. All these develop the subtle faculties of our heart and our inner or spiritual bodies. Development of our inner body brings many, many blessings. For example, through these practices we develop "inner muscles" and thus become less open to abuse from ourselves or others, and less open to addictions and obsessions of all kinds. When we become aware of our inner muscles—or bump into them, as has been my experience—it is a sign that our consciousness has been raised.

What do I mean by bumping into my inner muscles? There have been times when I have sensed that because of my spiritual practices I have been able to "move" or "bring into being" something that in the past I would not have been able to do. For example, I realize that I am letting go of something—perhaps worry or anger—faster than I used to, or I am more aware of a positive or negative attitude than I would have been in the past. When we can do this we are beginning to sense our inner muscles.

What is the fruit of all these things? Inner transformation and the release of our true inner light. For me this is summed up in the following statement by the American psychologist Gerald May:

> As your attachment ceases to be your motivation,
> your actions become expressions of divine love.[30]

The difficult part of this statement, of course, is being able to see or know what our attachments are. Eventually inner work helps us to see when we are attached—e.g., when we brace or when we cling. If we are aware of ourselves, we can most definitely sense it in our bodies. If we are aware of it in our heart, then we will be aware of it in our words and in our actions, and we will want to let go of the attachment. Gerald May goes on to quote a Tibetan Buddhist saying, which echoes his statement: "The more thy Soul unites with that which IS, the more thou wilt become COMPASSION ABSOLUTE."[31]

I believe these two similar statements express inner work at its best. That profound inner beauty can only be expressed in beautiful outer action, and we come to understand that our outer work truly is only as good as our inner work. We *know* when we are in the presence of divine love or compassion absolute. There is a freedom, space—the very best is brought out in us, and we too become the reflection of divine love. Likewise, sadly, we also know when we are in the presence of the opposite of compassion absolute. We brace, we cling, we become very defensive, and this leads to diminishment in our being and in our actions. Where a control freak is, love isn't.

When our actions become compassion absolute, we have left egoic thought (ordinary consciousness) behind and come to spiritual, even divine, consciousness. Thomas Keating uses a schematic diagram to convey these deepening forms of awareness. Rather than rings, Keating suggests we think of each level as shells. The outer shell is ordinary awareness, the second shell is spiritual awareness, the third shell is the true self, and the inner shell is the divine indwelling.

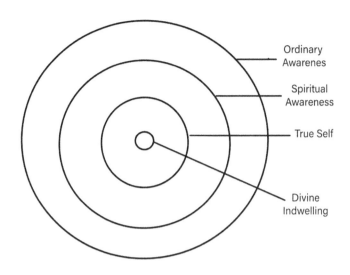

Ordinary
Awarenes

Spiritual
Awareness

True Self

Divine
Indwelling

I have found this diagram helpful when I am doing inner work. When I reflect on something that I have done or said, or that someone else has done or said, I ask, "Is this egoic awareness or spiritual awareness?" If I sense any inner bracing or clinging, I am in egoic awareness. If we can sense the difference between inner clinging/non-clinging and bracing/non-bracing we are on the path of inner awareness and inner work.

As alluded to earlier, differences between egoic and spiritual consciousness can be even more pronounced in groups. We have all had experiences when people listened to one another and there was a positive atmosphere. Sometimes, though, there can be animosity and outright hatred. Depending on what is being expressed, we can easily slip from one state of consciousness to another. If we are able to detach and sit back and watch this flow, it is fascinating. Simply through observation, we can learn how to live more in spiritual consciousness. The more we live in spiritual awareness, the more we notice things come together in beauty and harmony.

Learning how to detach is a basic wisdom lesson in the major religions. It seems to be very strong in the Buddhist religion in particular. When we talk about detachment, people in the West think it is about being cold, aloof, uncaring. But detachment in the Eastern sense means coming from a place beyond involvement in the outcome. And, as noted above, detachment is what we want if we are to become compassion absolute.

Remembering to notice or use the inner observer is key to inner work, and stepping into observer mode can shift us from intense identification to detachment. The following story offers a practical example of the use of the inner observer. During a contemplative retreat, a fellow retreatant, Judy, described once seeing a father and a screaming child in a parking lot. She said that instead of following her usual practice of making a snide remark to the father about poor parenting, she lifted the situation to God. Almost immediately the child stopped crying. Normally we might think that the "miracle" was that the child stopped crying, but it seems that the real miracle occurred when Judy saw that a different approach could be taken. When she thought to offer it to God, she stepped out of egoic consciousness or awareness and into spiritual awareness. Through Judy's new awareness, the situation changed. When we understand this, we can see, at a profound level, that indeed our outer work is only as good as our inner work. With a small inner shift, the true light in our hearts is released and amazing things happen on the outside. Buddhists would say Judy became awake.

One time I heard a crying child and decided to try what Judy did: I lifted the situation to God. To my chagrin, the child did not stop crying. This gave me an interior chuckle. The fact that I was able to laugh about it was an awakening in itself.

A few years ago I was at a three-day silent retreat. By the end of the retreat I realized how fragile my ego still was. I complained to myself, "I thought I had dealt with this. I thought I was beyond this." But the miracle was that I saw this fragility and realized I still needed to do more work, more healing. This seeing created a doorway to more healing, growth, and purification.

One of the most beautiful pieces of inner work I have read about is described in Malcolm Gladwell's *Outliers: The Story of Success.*

> In the 1960s, my mother wrote a book about her experiences. It was entitled *Brown Face, Big Master,* the "brown face" referring to herself, and the "big master" referring, in the Jamaican dialect, to God. At one point, she describes a time just after my parents [Malcolm's father was white, his mother mulatto] were married when they were living in London and my eldest brother was still a baby. They were looking for an apartment, and after a long search, my father found one in a London suburb. On the day after they moved in, however, the land lady ordered them out. "You didn't tell me your wife was Jamaican," she told my father in a rage.

In her book my mother describes her long struggle to make sense of this humiliation, to reconcile her experience with her faith. In the end, she was forced to acknowledge that anger was not an option and that as a colored Jamaican whose family had benefited for generations from the hierarchy of race, she could hardly reproach another for the impulse to divide people by the shade of their skin: [she writes]

> I complained to God in so many words: "Here I was, the wounded representative of the negro race in our struggle to be accounted free and equal with the dominating whites!" And God was amused; my prayer did not ring true with Him. I would try again. And then God said, "Have you not done the same thing? Remember this one you treated

less considerately than others because they were different superficially, and you were ashamed to be identified with them. Have you not been glad that you are not more colored than you are? Grateful that you are not black?" My anger and hate against the landlady melted. I was not better than she was, nor worse for that matter . . . We were both guilty of the sin of self-regard, the pride and the exclusiveness by which we cut some people off from ourselves.[32]

It took her a long time to get to a place of healing over this incident (I have found the same thing in my own life when I have faced challenges), but after much work she did it beautifully. We can see that her inner observer is present and her relationship with and trust in God shine through.

This is also an example of *thlipsis,* another aspect of spiritual work. Thlipsis is a Greek word meaning "compression" or "pressure." In a spiritual sense, thlipsis means purification or growth by friction. As we have all experienced, there are *many* opportunities for thlipsis when we are in community interacting with others! There have been times when I experienced particularly sharp thlipsis, and I have thought, "There is thlipsis and then there is torture." Sometimes it seems a fine line!

Many years ago I read in one of Corrie ten Boom's books about transforming jealousy. She suggests that when you feel jealous or envious of someone, you should thank God for that person's talent, good fortune, or whatever it is you are jealous of, and the jealousy will dissipate. On occasions when I have remembered to try this, especially if it is a superficial envy (and in a sense, all envy is superficial) I am feeling, the suggestion has always worked. I have found that simply being conscious that I am envious or jealous allows the feeling to dissolve. Why is this so? I think it is because the act of thanking God or even simply being aware of jealousy moves us from egoic consciousness to the spiritual. Through this we learn detachment.

Guilt is another emotion we struggle with. A saying of Thomas Keating has helped me enormously. He says, "If you're feeling guilt for more than thirty seconds you're being neurotic." Because of this statement, I am able to let go of guilt much more easily—it gives me permission!

When I'm emotionally upset about something, I find it extremely helpful to do something physical and repetitive—like the routine, physical work of cleaning the bathtub, or furiously pedaling on a bicycle or rowing on a rowing machine. The Benedictines know about this. Their motto *Ora et Labora* (Prayer and Work) is so important in inner work. Both occupations help redirect and dissipate the inner energy. Physical work also helps with conscious embodiment. That is, it gives us practice working with mindfulness and presence, sensing every part of our body in intentional action.

When I have discomfort in my body due to emotional situations, my reaction is to push it away. However, I have learned from Cynthia Bourgeault's teaching that when I feel discomfort in my body, I should hold on to the feeling so that I can ask my body "Where am I feeling this?" and "What exactly am I feeling?" I find I am better able to cope with the physical and emotional conditions when I do this because it can lead to a better understanding of what is really upsetting me and makes it easier for me to let go of the emotion when I am ready. From an inner perspective, I have found that an upside to having a body in pain or dis-ease is that it tends to make you more connected to and aware of your body. I find that when I am present in my body I am really present in the now. There is a part of me that longs to be disembodied when there is a lot of discomfort in my body. However, we have to have physical bodies on this plane of existence, and I'm really very glad to have the experience of being incarnate!

Listening to my body and being connected to it has most certainly helped me with inner work. I can think of a particular incident when I remembered to get connected to my body, even if it was belatedly. My dad and I were walking on a beautiful trail in Mount Douglas Park in the Victoria area when we ran into a man on his bike. Bikes were prohibited on that trail because of their very erosive impact. I challenged the man, and we got into a heated argument about the effects of bikes on the trail. My inner voice was telling me to walk away, but I was not listening to it. As we all know, but don't always put into practice, it is a mistake not to listen to your inner voice. I became so emotionally tied up that my stomach twisted into knots. I finally managed to walk away from the situation, but I still felt tight and shaken. Fortunately, the week before I had been at a Lenten workshop where the presenter talked about breathing away negativity. So using deep breaths I breathed the negativity away. Very soon I felt much less tight in my body, which enabled me to let go of the negative situation more easily.

Development of the inner observer is important for the healing of the ego. Eckhart Tolle, in his book *The Power of Now,* states that "the ego is the unobserved mind." Through the simple observance of our thoughts, we are much less likely to say or do self-centred or unkind things. Even if we use our inner observer after the fact, we can learn from it. For example, after we do or say something unkind, if we use the inner observer we will know what we did wasn't helpful or healing. If mindfulness and prayer are present, a different outcome is more likely to occur. It is all a learning experience. There will be more chances!

American psychologist John Welwood has an interesting and beautiful view of the ego:

> Our ego itself is testimony to the force of love. It developed as a way to keep going in the face of perceived threats to our existence, primarily lack of love. In the places where love was missing, we built ego defenses. So every time we enact one of

our defensive behaviours we are implicitly paying
homage to love as the most important thing.[33]

Another practice that helps inner work is *lectio divina*. When
we listen to a biblical reading in church, we are usually on
to the next part of the service before we can even partially
digest what we have heard. With *lectio divina* there are periods
of silence between the scripture readings, which allow the
inner teachings to be taken in and worked on at the level of
the heart. Absorbing the readings this way is akin to water
dripping onto a stone, drop by drop, and the stone acting like
a sponge, rather than having the water quickly splash onto and
over the rock. In *lectio divina*, after a Bible passage has been
read two or three times, with a few minutes of silence between
each reading, people are invited to say out loud a word or
phrase that particularly struck them. A new reality comes out
of this profound encounter or relationship with scripture. The
same thing happens in profound encounters with great pieces
of music, art, or literature, or ultimately with a great spiritual
master, such as Jesus.

As suggested by Gerald May's statement, quoted earlier,
we can become expressions of divine love by learning how
to surrender to God and empty ourselves (a process known as
kenosis). For Christians, Jesus is the ultimate in self-emptying
as he allowed people to take him away and nail him to a cross.
Logion 42 in the *Gospel of Thomas* describes self-emptying
beautifully: "Come into being as you pass away." As the
resurrection of Jesus underlines, he could not help but come
into being as he passed away. Another way of looking at it is
that Jesus was so raised in being that his being was raised for
those who loved him.

For Christians, Lent is the perfect season for inner work and
self-emptying. The words in the liturgy for the Ash Wednesday

service—"Dust you are and to dust you shall return"—clearly speak to kenosis and the larger picture.

In *Three Cups of Tea,* Greg Mortenson and David Relin tell a marvellous story of a wise headman who lets go and self-empties so that he can see the larger picture and become compassion absolute. Mortenson led a group that built schools in rural Pakistan and Afghanistan. When his group had almost completed its first school, Haji Mehdi, the headman (and thug) of another village showed up with his henchmen at Korphe, the village where the school was being built, and said, "Allah forbids the education of girls. And I forbid the construction of this school."

> "We will finish our school," Haji Ali [the Korphe headman] said evenly. "Whether you forbid it or not." After some uneasy moments and discussion Mehdi said, "I demand twelve of your largest rams."
>
> "As you wish," Haji Ali said, turning his back on Mehdi, to emphasize how he had degraded himself by demanding a bribe. [This demand and accession greatly distressed everyone in the village, especially each family's oldest boy, whose job it was to look after the animals, which were their most cherished possessions.]

"It was one of the most humbling things I've ever seen," Mortenson wrote. "Haji Ali had just handed over half the wealth of the village to that crook, but he was smiling like he'd just won the lottery." Later Haji Ali told the villagers, "Don't be sad. Long after all those rams are dead and eaten this school will still stand. Haji Mehdi has food today. Now our children have education forever."[34]

The profound wisdom of Haji Ali shines through this story, a triumph of light over darkness. Who knows where this story may go? Maybe because of schools like the one in Korphe there will one day be no more behaviour like that displayed by Haji Mehdi.

When we are spiritually transformed, we create a less virulent environment. Evolutionary biologists and epidemiologists know that the less virulent the environment, the less potent the disease will be. As the English cleric Martin Israel says, to have a clean physical environment we must have a clean psychic environment. I believe that as our inner world is purified, our outer world will be too, not only in how we care for one another, but also in how we care for all creation. As it says in the *Bhagavad Gita*:

> When these [fleeting things like heat and cold,
> pleasure and pain] cannot torment a man,
> when suffering and joy are equal
> for him and he has courage,
> he is fit for immortality.[35]

This is the fruit of self-emptying. I am still working on it!

Spiritual growth is not an easy thing, but because of spiritual evolution, described in "The Progression of Consciousness," I believe it is becoming more accessible. With accessibility, new vistas of the spirit open up. These new vistas allow us to see and work at greater depth, and thus be more raised in being. As a result, greater inner healing can occur, more self-emptying can take place, and nothing short of compassion absolute is reflected. Ultimately this can lead to unitive (non-dual) seeing, where we are aware of seeing the oneness of everything. This is probably the closest we can come to an infinite "God's view" with our finite minds.

I cannot stress enough the importance of inner or spiritual work. As we grow on the interior, we find we have more options, more freedom, and are more helpful to the cosmos. This work transforms the world because it is how we come to see the kingdom of God on Earth. Inner work leads to self-emptying, which was crucial to the work of Jesus and is crucial to our work.

A few last thoughts on inner work:

> As long as you derive inner help and comfort from anything, keep it.
>
> Gandhi

> The one and only test of a valid religious idea, doctrinal statement, spiritual experience, or devotional practice was that it must lead directly to practical compassion.
>
> Karen Armstrong, *The Spiral Staircase*

> The outward work
> will never be puny
> if the inward work
> is great.
> And the outward work
> can never be great or even good
> if the inward one is puny or of little worth.
> The inward work invariably
> includes in itself
> all expansiveness,
> all breadth,
> all length,
> all depth.
> Such work
> receives and draws all its being
> from nowhere else except
> from and in the heart of God.
>
> Meister Eckhart[36]

The statements by Karen Armstrong and Meister Eckhart both express that the fruits of true inner work are actions which express divine love—compassion absolute.

THE UNRECOGNIZED
GIFT OF SILENCE

Be still, and know that I am God.

Psalm 46:10

Nothing in all creation is so like God as silence.

Meister Eckhart

Only silence can reach that dimension of reality that is too deep for words.

Thomas Merton, *Paradise Journey*

Silence is not the absence of noise, it's the absence of resistance.

Cynthia Bourgeault

Truth—is the offspring of silence, unbroken meditation.

Sir Isaac Newton

I call silence the unrecognized gift because we humans frequently ignore it and give very little space to it in our lives. Yet silence is where the spirit does its work. The spiritual masters quoted above know and knew this well. From my experience, silence can be one of the most potent tools for healing and consciousness raising. As St. John of the Cross says, silence is God's first language. In John's Gospel, Pilate asks Jesus at his interrogation, "What is truth?" (John 18:38). There is no record of Jesus's reply; perhaps he gave the perfect answer to that question—silence.

The practice of silence has always held a central place in the worship of the Quakers. It is no coincidence that the Quakers have often been at the forefront of a kinder, gentler world. They have been the outliers for the abolition of slavery and capital punishment, the emancipation of women, and the end of exploitation of all kinds, including of the environment.

I once heard a very talkative woman in my church community say that it wasn't in her nature to be silent. I wish I'd had the presence of being to say gently that maybe it was because she didn't know her true nature. At a deep level I believe we are all natural contemplatives, and all natural mystics.

When we go into silence, the ego is shifted out of the driver's seat so that we can move to deeper levels of consciousness. When I said this to my clergy friend Kevin, he replied, "To get the ego out of the driver's seat, you must stop the car." How do we stop the car? In a phrase—silence and stillness. Psalm 46:10 has been saying this across the ages. The spiritual masters say that silence is *essential* to spiritual work and transformation. We need to take this much more to heart.

Silence is the doorway to the inner world. In *Meditations on the Tarot,* Valentin Tomberg says, "Silence is the sign of real contact with the spiritual world and this contact, in turn, always engenders the influx of forces."[37] I have found this to be true. Nature does abhor a vacuum. Something happens during silence. We sink below the surface; we sense and live at a deeper level. As Herman Melville has noted, "All profound things are preceded and attended by silence." On silent retreats, I find that I come to know fellow retreatants in a different way, a deeper way. In silence I have a keener sense of each person's energy. Silence gives that gift.

One of my most amazing experiences with silence occurred at a Lenten study group. During the evening we had a break in the program and were told we could either have tea and coffee in the hall or go into the church for fifteen or twenty minutes of silence. About two-thirds of the group chose to be in silence in the church. After the break the program resumed, and I sensed a group calmness, cohesion, and unity that was extraordinary. This ethos had certainly not been present before. It was the power of silence and real contact with the spiritual world that created this presence or, as the Buddhists would call it, mindfulness.

On another occasion, the rector of St. George's, Cadboro Bay, decided to have a contemplative Eucharist at the main Sunday service. Even the brief silences during the service had a profound effect. One member of the congregation came into the sanctuary just before the Eucharist. After the service she asked, "What did you do to those people?" There was a depth and emotion that had not been there before. Other congregants commented on how beautiful and meaningful the service was.

The Contemplative Society always begins its meetings with at least ten minutes of silence. At Contemplative Society board meetings we often stop the meeting partway through and have ten more minutes of silence. The subtle yet intense shift is marvellous to experience and can have a profound effect on the course of the meeting. Things unfold in a way they would not have done had we foregone the few minutes of silence. I think it would be a terrific idea if all meetings began with ten minutes of silence and stopped midway for silence. Such meetings would take on a life of their own and develop in unexpected and good ways.

To help remind us of the importance of silence, here is a wonderful prayer from the Iona Community:

> When the world tells us
> we are what we do with our activity, acumen, or achievement,
> let us learn
> WE ARE WHAT WE DO WITH OUR SILENCE.
>
> When the world tells us
> we are what we do with our spending power, selling power, or our power of speech, let us learn
> WE ARE WHAT WE DO WITH OUR SILENCE.
>
> When the world tells us to drown the silent sufferings of others with indifference or noise,
> or forget the art of stillness even in the storm,
> let us learn
> WE ARE WHAT WE DO WITH OUR SILENCE.
>
> When the world tells us
> to rush in where angels fear to tread,
> let us learn that angels listen first
> before they take a step
> for the voice of God in the silence . . . [38]

In his book *Medicine Walk*, Richard Wagamese miraculously brings the deep mysticism, stillness, and silence of all the true religions/spiritualities of the world together in his description of a man learning to track game. The final sentence of the paragraph could also describe a person who is completely at one with deep inner silence and stillness.

> The old man showed him how to slip between trees like a shadow. He taught him to move with exquisite slowness, almost not like moving at all, so

that every inch of forward motion seemed to take a year. He learned how to wrap himself in shadow, how to stoop and crawl between rocks and logs, how to hide himself in plain sight. He learned to stand or sit or lay in one position for hours. He could slow his breathing so that even in the chill air of winter the exhalations could be barely seen. He learned how to go inward, how to become whole in his stillness and forget the very nature of time.[39]

Silence is a prerequisite to any form of contemplative prayer or inner transformation. The next chapter explores my favourite form of contemplative prayer: centering prayer, or resting in (the silence of) God.

The only tyrant I accept in this world is the still voice within.

Gandhi

CENTERING PRAYER

I now descend into the cave of my heart to be one
with you.

Edward Hays, *Prayers for a Planetary Pilgrim*

. . . for a naked intent direct to God is sufficient
without anything else.

The Cloud of Unknowing

. . . at the still point, there the dance is.

T.S. Eliot, "Burnt Norton," *Four Quartets*

There are two kinds of prayer. Anyone who has ever
said or thought a prayer has participated in cataphatic
prayer—prayer with form. Apaphatic prayer is prayer
without form. A better way to explain the difference between
cataphatic prayer and apaphatic prayer is to think of cataphatic
prayer as prayer that uses the faculties (i.e., memory, reason,
imagination), and apaphatic prayer as prayer that does not
use the faculties. Church liturgy is virtually all cataphatic,
but it is truly amazing that even in a few moments of silence
the apaphatic can become manifest and can resonate deep
within us.

I have heard people in my church community say "I pray
while I'm driving" or "I pray while I'm walking the dog." That
is fine for intercessory and other forms of cataphatic prayer, but

it is much less effective for apaphatic forms of prayer, and is less likely to produce inner transformation.

This is not to diminish cataphatic prayer at all. Madeleine L'Engle said that every prayer is an act of love. I believe this. I am aware of many instances where intercessory prayer was very effective and did much good. I believe that "no conscious thought is lost."[40] One of my most startling experiences with intercessory prayer occurred when I was in the hospital's emergency room. As I did not know what the doctors were going to "do" to me and was very anxious I had high blood pressure. I suddenly felt uplifted and not nearly so anxious. I learned later that this was about the time a prayer chain of people had started praying for me. Many, many people are witnesses to the wonderful, positive fruits of intercessory prayer.

A prerequisite to any kind of prayer is silence. Jesus frequently went to deserted places to pray (see Luke 5:16, for example). His wise words should be heeded: "When you pray, go into your room and shut the door" (Matthew 6:6). On one level, this statement means that people should not make a show of their prayer and, literally, should shut the door on outer noise and commotion. At an inner and deeper level it can be interpreted as a command to go into the room of your heart. This is essential advice for apaphatic prayer *and* spiritual transformation.

In 1977 I joined a prayer group that I found very stimulating. The format was a mixture of Bible study, discussion, and intercessory prayer. Although there were short periods of silence—that is, apaphatic prayer—there was also much talk, so the group was overwhelmingly cataphatic in nature. I learned much from many of the people in the group, and I grew spiritually. By the early 1990s, however, I was becoming dissatisfied. The discussions seemed confining rather than expansive, and I felt the group was no longer helping me grow. In hindsight, I realize I was looking for something deeper— silent, apaphatic prayer was calling me. Eventually the group disbanded; perhaps we had all grown and evolved beyond the original vision.

I tried Christian meditation, but the practice of using a mantra never suited me. Saying a mantra over and over seemed too much work for me. I wanted something simpler, where I could sink down into silence and just be. Then I heard about praying in silence, which led me to centering prayer. In 1994 I heard Cynthia Bourgeault speak for the first time. I knew I was listening to something special. I had never heard someone speak of spirituality and faith with such depth and quality. After that encounter, I began to explore the practice of centering prayer and have found it indispensable for my spiritual growth and inner work.

The modern form of centering prayer was developed in the 1970s by a group of Trappist monks at St. Joseph's Abbey in Spencer, Massachusetts,[41] although its roots go back much further. An antecedent can be found in Chapter 7 of *The Cloud of Unknowing,* a book written by an anonymous English mystic in the late fourteenth century, and the Desert Fathers of the fourth century certainly practised a form of contemplative prayer.

Essentially, centering prayer is consenting to rest in God for twenty to twenty-five minutes. Practitioners choose a sacred word or a short phase—for example, "Come, Lord," "Peace," or "Trust love"—so that when they notice their thoughts wandering, they can gently bring themselves back to the word or short phrase and rest or centre in God. There is a wonderful story told about Thomas Keating when he was at a workshop teaching centering prayer. A woman came up to him and said, "Father Thomas, I am no good at centering prayer. I have had 10,000 thoughts while practicing it." Without missing a beat Thomas said, "How wonderful, you had 10,000 chances to return to God."

Cynthia Bourgeault has described centering prayer as the perfect wisdom practice. When we notice our thoughts have been wandering, we wake up and come to attention. By saying our sacred word, we return to God/our centre/love and surrender. According to Cynthia, attention and surrender are the two mainstays of wisdom (see Introduction).

Thomas Keating remarks that in centering prayer we "take a vacation from our thoughts." It is as if for once our hearts are training our minds. The practice changes not so much *what* we think but *how* we think. To use a technological metaphor, it is like a change in a computer operating system. During prayer periods we can switch from an egoic operating system to a spiritual operating system (see Keating's "shells of consciousness" diagram on page 33). However, Cynthia Bourgeault notes that "only gradually does [centering prayer] create the changes whereby the egoic operating system ceases to be our chief mode of perceiving the world and Spiritual Awareness stabilizes as a consistent Attention of the Heart, the physiological undergirding of nondual consciousness."[42]

Christopher Page writes:

> In silent prayer we do not try to accomplish anything or to persuade God to do something for us or for the world. We are not trying to build even God's kingdom. For a few moments we are resting in the miracle of not trying. We are practicing letting go, and as we let go, we enter into the deep wellspring of God's mercy. We are at peace in that place, learning to trust the flow of God's mercy.
>
> We cannot think our way to this state of rest. Good works will not get us there. Workshops, discussion groups, even Bible study, will not bring us to the land of transparent trust in the mercy of God. We get to this place of rest and trust only by resting and trusting.[43]

In contemplative prayer, we listen to God in interior connectedness. As the spiritual teacher Adyashanti says, "There is a part of you that is always still, always silent, always meditating."[44] It is in these silent depths that our heart connects with God. At first it is a place we visit; then it becomes the person we are. The closer we go to the centre, the more we become "oned" with God. At this depth we often cannot sense the work that is being done—we may never be fully aware of it, or we may not notice it until much later. There are times when we might be able to say something has changed, but my experience is that such times are rare.

Centering prayer is a form of contemplative prayer. It creates more space inside us by placing us in spiritual consciousness rather than in the small space of egoic consciousness that we are almost always in. This shift in consciousness creates changes in our thinking and being, which in turn affect our saying and doing.

When we practise centering prayer, perhaps over years, purification comes, the pain centre and defences relax, emotions well up, and long-forgotten memories are healed. The practice helps us develop excellent inner work habits that seep into our exterior lives in many ways. As we learn to let go of our thoughts during prayer time, we develop "a capacity to stabilize inner observation as a proclivity of the heart, and to carry this noticing into daily life without an overly mental mindfulness."[45] We become keener and deeper observers of what is going on around us. This develops sensitivity, which in turn develops awareness. And when we become aware, we are simply more engaged in life.

The beautiful rhythm that centering prayer creates can be seen in the life of Jesus: Jesus withdraws in prayer and then goes out in service. As Thich Nhat Hanh, the Buddhist monk who coined the phrase "socially engaged Buddhism," says, "Don't just do something, sit there." He explains, "With all this socially engaged work, . . . first you must learn what the Buddha learned, to still the mind. Then you don't take action; action takes you."[46]

At deep levels of contemplation we may engage in what is known as the prayer of the heart. According to Lynn Bauman,

> Christian spirituality describes many levels of prayer, one of which is the Prayer of the Heart. When an individual begins to descend below the level of mental prayer and finds a place of awareness deep within (at the level of the heart), and begins to pray there, he or she is said to have entered the Prayer of the Heart. This is not one simple or easy step, it itself is a journey into an immense territory as vast as the universe itself, for the ocean of Infinity laps at the shores of the heart.[47]

This statement of Lynn's dovetails with Kabir Helminski's description of the heart as "a vast realm of mind that includes psychic and extrasensory abilities; intuition; wisdom; a sense of unity; aesthetic, qualitative, and creative faculties; and image-forming and symbolic capacities."[48]

Thomas Keating says of centering prayer:

> The regular practice of contemplative prayer initiates a healing process that might be called the "divine therapy." The level of deep rest accessed during the prayer periods loosens up the hard-pan around the emotional weeds stored in the unconscious, of which the body seems to be the warehouse. The psyche begins to evacuate spontaneously the undigested emotional material of a lifetime, opening up new space for self-knowledge, freedom of choice, and the discovery of the divine presence within. As a consequence, a growing trust in God, a bonding with the Divine Therapist, enable us to endure the process.

Thus, the gift of contemplative prayer is a practical and essential tool for confronting the heart of the Christian ascesis—namely, the struggle with our unconscious motivation—while at the same time establishing the climate and necessary dispositions for a deepening relationship with God and leading, if we persevere, to divine union.[49]

Here, Thomas Keating talks about "the struggle with our unconscious motivation," which reflects directly on Gerald May's statement: "As your attachment ceases to be your motivation, your actions become expressions of divine love." As our unconscious motivations are purified, absolute compassion is made more and more manifest in us.

Selinde Krayenhoff, a former board member of the Contemplative Society, and now an Anglican priest, has some excellent, practical thoughts on her practice of centering prayer:

I'm not perfect at Centering Prayer. I don't have to be. It's a practice, not a goal. Like the prodigal son, I return to it over and over. When I miss a few days or a week, I don't get bogged down with self-recrimination. That just prolongs the agony. All I have to do is show up. I don't pretend to know what God is doing during my prayer time. It's not my business. My work is to simply show up. And to state my intention. What is my intention? It's important that I'm clear. My intention is to invite God's presence and action in my life. And as soon as I sit down, I notice how I *long* for God's presence and action in my life. And it's all a miracle to me how my life continues to unfold.[50]

Selinde also makes clear the direct connection between Jesus and centering prayer:

> Centering Prayer prepares us for this reality of the constant letting go in life. How? For twenty minutes every morning, I practice my "letting go" muscle. How do I do this? As I sit in prayer, every time a thought comes up, I let it go. And briefly return to my sacred word. That word, a short phrase really, reminds me of my intention—to sit quietly with God. Over and over, every day, I practice this letting go of thoughts. And if I get confused about why I'm practicing in this way, I think of Jesus. His life was not a spiritual practice that ended up in peace and contentment. No, his was a life of surrender. In the end, he let go fully . . . on the cross—in total surrender. Jesus is the master of letting go and teaches us, through example, the power of letting go.[51]

While we are on the topic of letting go; I was sent some beautiful sayings put on a sign at a gas station by owner Alison Billett of Johannesburg, South Africa:

> When you forgive you heal.
> When you let go you grow.

It can be so challenging for us to forgive and to let go, but I have found that there is so much wisdom in these statements. When you use your letting go muscle over and over in centering prayer, letting go becomes easier. So it is with forgiveness.

If I'm in the midst of a busy time, I may go for up to a week without practising centering prayer. I always get the feeling, though, that I'm beginning to stray off course and that I need to get centred in God again. Retreats are wonderful because they give me the opportunity to intensively practice centering prayer, perhaps doing as much as three hours a day. With this amount of prayer, one needs spiritual and psychological support, which is present at a retreat. I also find when practising centering prayer in a group that while there can be distraction from the presence of people, the support I feel helps me to be more focused.

As I have continued over the years to practise centering prayer, I have come to experience several things. For one, it may seem as though there are times when I sense I am getting nowhere. I try to remember Thomas Keating's assurance: "The only way you can fail at prayer is to fail to show up." The practice may have a calming effect or be very disruptive. Many times I have found myself letting go of negative memories or thoughts of negative situations that are definitely not serving me or the world in a positive way. This is all part of the purification process, which Keating refers to as "the archaeological dig." Resting in deep silence takes us into the depths of God, to healing and transformation and glimpses of "infinitely more than we can ask or imagine."[52]

Through centering prayer, I have experienced many times the healing that can take place in the interior world. Early in my practice I had a vision. It was not a pleasant experience. I sensed that I had disturbed a frightening and horrible monster. The vision reminded me of the dwarves in *The Lord of the Rings* who dug too deeply in the mines of Moria and disturbed the Balrog, a hideous monster who eventually drove them from the mines. I felt that I had dug too deeply, but with God present all was well. Eventually I realized that this vision was almost certainly a sign that something deep was being released and healed. (I speak more about healing in the next chapter.)

During a centering prayer session we may be unaware that any healing has taken place, or we may not know what exactly has been healed, but if we experience a sense of uneasiness, be assured that something is going on at deep levels. Being attentive to these subtleties is an excellent way to hone our inner awareness.

One time, I attended a meeting that deeply disturbed me. I found myself brooding obsessively over what was said and what I might say to the person who was the main irritant the next time we met. I decided that every time I had a thought about the meeting over the next twenty-four hours, I would do what I practise in centering prayer and let the thought go. I was appalled by the amount of time and energy I spent thinking of that situation. Each time it brought up emotions of anger and frustration in me. It often seemed that I no sooner let go of the thought than I found myself thinking about the situation again. After more than a day of this I was mentally exhausted. It was a very revealing exercise that helped me grow and taught me several things. It gave my inner muscles quite a workout, and I learned that I still had much work to do on letting go of disturbing/negative thoughts and situations. I did not banish the experience of the meeting from my thoughts, but I did come to realize that I didn't have to be swept away on a raging flood of my anger and fear. If you feel ready, try this exercise. Be prepared to be mentally exhausted and perhaps frustrated!

On occasion I have felt too upset to settle in centering prayer. When this happens, I acknowledge the emotions I feel and then practise a slow walking meditation, which I find helpful.

> What we plant in the soil of contemplation, we shall reap in the harvest of action.
>
> Meister Eckhart

> . . . at the still point, there the dance is.
>
> T.S. Eliot, "Burnt Norton," *Four Quartets*

That statement says it all! The still point is indeed where the dance is. People who practise contemplative prayer or meditation understand this. The still point may seem like nothing, but it is where the cosmos unfolds.

> Prayer from the heart can achieve what nothing else
> can in the world.
>
> Gandhi

HEALING

The only true spiritual power is the power of healing.

John Dominic Crossan

A central aspect of Jesus's ministry on earth was the shamanistic or healing abilities that he brought forth into the physical world. The people of Jesus's time swarmed to him because of these abilities, and the stories of healings that occurred in Jesus's presence excite and intrigue me most about Jesus. All my life I have asked "How did he do this?"

But this question leads us astray. Jesus did not "do" the healing. He was the vehicle for healing, and it was the presence and recognition of God at work in him. Those who were healed in his presence recognized something in him. "Deep calls to deep" as Psalm 42:7 puts it. Something deep in the people being healed resonated with something deep in Jesus.

The healings and resurrections that occurred in the presence of Jesus are astounding, and because they are astounding many people simply dismiss them. Sadly, even some Christians do not believe in spiritual or energy healing. Several years ago my mother was part of the healing committee at our church. When they did a congregational survey, someone wrote "Healing isn't for everyone." In exasperation my mother said, "Next they're going to say God isn't for everyone."

I don't believe I have ever met a person who was not in need of some kind of healing, and I know I have never met a person who did not have the potential to be healed. Such is the oneness of God. Since we are in God (there is nothing outside), we can all receive healing.

If we are not healed, have we failed? Absolutely not. Intention is paramount. To quote Rafe Robbin OSB: "No conscious thought is lost." So it is not a failure. The cure will come. Our seeking and striving for a cure are all part of the healing and creation process of the universe.

At one time I remember thinking that to heal via science was fantastic, but it would be even more fantastic to reach out and make people whole via the spiritual route. I heard an inner voice say "They are one and the same thing."

So now when I think of the two types of physical healing, energetic/spiritual and scientific, I understand them this way: to heal via science means we can cure *any* case of a *particular* disease; to heal via spirit/energy means we can cure *any* disease on a case by case (*particular*) basis (scientific medicine is just beginning to get into particular healing by designing cures according to a particular person's DNA). The two routes of healing are different, but the result is the same. They cure a disease or heal an injury because each in their own way gets to the root of the problem. And to understand the root cause of a disease, a level of either spiritual or scientific awareness/consciousness is attained.

To illustrate this, if a doctor from today travelled through time and cured someone from the 1860s using modern medicine, anyone who witnessed the cure would think the doctor was a god or a magician. But the difference is just that we've reached a higher level of scientific awareness, we now know about germs and antibiotics and cancer cells, etc. Similarly, we still think of Jesus's cures as miraculous because we have not yet reached that level of spiritual awareness where scientific and spiritual healing merge. Spiritual understanding has greatly increased from where it was 2,000 years ago, and this is manifested in an outer way by more awareness, openness, and, most importantly, compassion. We still have a long way to go, but it's clear to me that spiritual transformation plays a vital role in the healing and unfolding of our planet and our cosmos.

For spiritual healing to occur, I think both healer and healed need to consent or surrender to divine love—that is, they must enter into a unitive or non-dual consciousness. Unitive or non-dual consciousness can be defined as "seeing from oneness," or "no-separation." There is an old joke about non-dual consciousness:

> "What did the mystic say to the hot-dog vendor?"
> "Make me one with everything."

When Cynthia Bourgeault is pressed to explain non-duality, she begins by saying what duality is: subject/object, black/white, this not that. She says that non-dual consciousness is perception *from* oneness not *of* oneness.

> At times this unitive seeing may sweep you up into rapt adoration; at other times it simply deposits you powerfully and nakedly in the present moment. Either form is an expression of the same underlying consciousness. It is this consciousness itself that is the attained state of contemplation, and it is neither infused nor acquired, because it was never absent— only unrecognized.[53]

The concept of non-dual consciousness as it applies to healing is beautifully stated by Arthur Guirdham in his book *The Nature of Healing*:

> The fusion of two souls which occurs in healing is really a return to the universal consciousness in

which disease is impossible. It is a re-entering on the part of both, of the common consciousness of the universe. The fusion of their two souls is merely a reflection in microcosm of the macrocosm of the universal consciousness.[54]

We often think of Jesus as being the "whole show" in the miracles of the Gospels. However, without those people in whom Jesus was able to manifest the kingdom of God, healing could not have occurred. Jesus may have been the ultimate musical player, but those encountering him were the fabulous instruments.

A hot area in medical investigation at present is stem cell research, which uses undifferentiated human cells that could become any kind of cell that is needed for healing. Stem cell therapy takes things back to the beginning, and on the physical level it sounds very much like "a return to the universal consciousness in which disease is impossible."

But the real leap in healing will come when we are able to heal from the inside—that is, when we are able to harness energy/spiritual healing.

There are hints of healing energy recorded in the Gospels. I think of the story of a woman who had hemorrhaged for twelve years (Mark 5:25-34). There were people pressing all around Jesus, trying to touch him so they could receive healing, and the woman came up behind him and touched his cloak, believing, correctly, that if she only touched him, she would be healed. Jesus immediately noticed that someone had been healed because the power had gone out of him.

Two instances of energy/spiritual healing in my own life stand out in my mind. One involved the laying on of hands. In the Christian tradition this is done by people who are drawn or called to healing, who with prayer lay their hands on the head or the shoulders of a person who asks for this rite. During a healing service at Christ Church Cathedral in Victoria, I went to the altar along with dozens of other people for this sacrament. The two people, one clergy, one lay, who performed the rite were fairly experienced. I remember their hands hovered a few inches over my head rather than being placed directly on it, and I felt a gentle tingling throughout my body, beginning at my head and ending as an extraordinary sensation of something lightly curling and feathering in my feet.

I have also had experiences with Reiki healing, which I regard as an intensive form of laying on of hands. As Reiki practitioner Eileen Curteis SSA writes,

> Similar to the Christian laying on of hands, Reiki is like a prayer over the entire body bringing peace, harmony and well-being. In my daily practice of Reiki, the recipient is invited to surrender to the living God within one's energy system, thereby activating the body's natural ability to heal. It is not the practitioner's energy but God's that does the healing.[55]

One of Sister Eileen's Reiki colleagues, Elizabeth, is my Reiki therapist and also a member of my church community. Over the years I have had many sessions with her. After I lie down on a comfortable therapy table, Elizabeth always begins with prayer while I either pray or try to enter into a relaxed, meditative state. Elizabeth was also trained in massage, and I love the massage even more than the Reiki treatment. After treatment, to complete the wonderful experience, she warms a robe and socks in the dryer, and I luxuriate in them in an easy chair while we drink tea, eat muffins, and chat. What a blessing! Many times after the Reiki treatment my arthritis is less painful.

Sister Eileen notes that "often the receiver feels heat from the practitioner's hands although sometimes it is experienced as a cool soothing energy depending on the needs of the body."[56] I have felt heat in various parts of my body many times while undergoing Reiki, and Elizabeth confirms that she feels heat in the same parts of her body when she is giving me the treatment.

I have heard many wonderful stories of healing with Reiki, some of them at an evening gathering at the Sisters of St. Ann's Queenswood Centre, where Sister Eileen and others spoke about this form of treatment. In one story, a Reiki practitioner said to the person she was treating, "There is an extremely cold spot right here in your back." The patient replied that a few years earlier she had had a cancerous lump removed at that spot. This evening at Queeenswood was very special to me. About 100 people attended, and there was such a presence of love in the space that healing was there. My arthralgia felt almost non-existent in that space.

All these experiences with energy healing are small examples of what Jesus manifested much more completely. Eileen Curteis has written:

> As we move through the new millennium, I believe that we are going to explore the frontiers of healing in a whole new way and that Reiki is just one of them. I believe holistic healing will be one of the great adventures of our century and for those of us who have the courage to embark on it, we will each in our turn be trail blazers who leave a legacy for the generations to come. It is together in community we make our journey.[57]

Sister Eileen is quite right. I believe frontiers of healing are being explored in a whole (pun intended!) new way. In his book *Vistas of Infinity: How to Enjoy Life When You Are Dead*, Jurgen Ziewe recounts healing during lucid dreaming while out of his physical body.

> It has long been argued and proven that healing can be found using lucid dreams or Out-of-Body experiences.

When we moved house a few years ago I pulled a muscle in my groin lifting furniture. I was in a lot of pain and found it difficult to move without the pain taking my breath away.

On the third day, in the early hours of the morning [sounds like there's going to be a resurrection!] during meditation I was able to leave my body and found myself seeing it from the outside, sitting there in my meditation chair, with my head tilted slightly forward, seemingly asleep. On the left side of my groin I saw a six-inch black hole with dark particles gyrating randomly and chaotically around inside it. I immediately identified it as the trouble spot that had given me so much pain. Not being able to think of anything better to do, I used my Out-of-Body hands and gently pulled the hole shut, while at the same time sending positive energy into it. Gradually the hole closed and the dark energy dissipated, and soon the dark spot had disappeared completely. I decided to return to my body in order to check whether this was just a hallucination or whether I had actually closed the "hole" and by doing so eradicated the problem. When I opened my physical eyes the pain had completely gone. I got up, moved around, twisted my body, there was not a trace of any pain.[58]

I believe healing in the future may look much more like this. In fact, it is already happening. How marvellous!

Suffering any kind of disease is so terrible that we must work diligently in the physical as well as spiritual realms to overcome incurable diseases that still exist on the Earth. I believe the communion of saints in the unseen realm helps in subtle and profound ways, smoothing pathways and causing "coincidences" to happen. If we have the ability to see these subtleties and coincidences, we can act. The more people who help in any way will expedite the healing of the world. Oh, the rejoicing in the heaven of our hearts!

Even if we cannot be healed, there can still be good news. In the Gospels, Christ says that Bartimaeus was born blind that he might see the grace of God. I used to find this statement shocking. I was indignant that this man suffered so much, but gradually, as my spiritual journey deepened, I began to understand that being able to see the grace of God was more wonderful than any suffering. In fact, having the ability to see the grace or the love of God despite any affliction is far greater than any suffering. It is like being carried across the river of suffering in the boat of love.

MYSTICAL EXPERIENCES

> Mystical states however, are never merely interruptive. They leave behind a residue that modifies the inner life of the person.
>
> William James, *The Varieties of Religious Experience*

> . . . direct inner experience, the most potent teacher of all.
>
> Keely Bays[59]

People sometimes call mystical or metaphysical experiences supernatural (above nature). I don't see it that way. As Ken Wilber points out, what people in the past took to be supernatural is in fact intranatural (within nature). As our consciousness grows, we become able to see that things are really part of a whole. Nothing is outside nature; we may just not yet understand the natural laws that explain it.

Non-Dual Experiences

> All mystical practices are designed to dispel this pernicious illusion of separateness.
>
> Timothy Freke[60]

> Our separation from each other is an illusion of consciousness.
>
> Albert Einstein

Within its depths I saw ingathered, bound by love
in one mass, the scattered leaves of the universe:
substance and accidents and their relations, as
though together fused, so that what I speak of is one
simple flame. The universal form of this complex
I think I saw, because, as I say this, more largely I
feel myself rejoice.

Dante Alighieri, *Il Paradiso*

Timothy Freke describes Christian mysticism this way:

Mysticism is the spiritual essence of Christianity.
The mystics are not content to have a relationship
with God via priests and institutions, but look inside
themselves to know God directly. When they do,
God is revealed as an all-embracing love that unites
the universe into one indivisible whole.[61]

Seeing the universe as an indivisible whole is a mystical
experience found in all faiths.

To me, mystical experiences seem to be variations on the
non-dual or unitive experience, which I consider the most
holistic of all mystical experiences. With a unitive experience I
sense that I come closest to perceiving the consciousness of God.

In the poem "Vacillation," W.B. Yeats describes the
experience well:

My fiftieth year had come and gone,
I sat, a solitary man,
In a crowded London shop,
An open book and empty cup
On the marble table-top.

While on the shop and street I gazed
My body of a sudden blazed,
And twenty minutes more or less

It seemed, so great my happiness,
That I was blessed and could bless.

As does Elizabeth Goudge in the following passage from *The White Witch*:

> . . . she had long accepted the fact that happiness is like swallows in spring. It may come and nest under your eaves or it may not. You cannot command it. When you expect to be happy you are not, when you don't expect to be happy there is suddenly Easter in your soul, though it be midwinter. Something, you do not know what, has broken the seal upon that door in the depth of your being that opens upon eternity. It is not yet time for you yourself to go out of it but what is beyond comes in and passes into you and through you.

One of the best-known descriptions of a non-dual experience is from Thomas Merton. It does not surprise me that this is one of the most often quoted passages from Merton's writing.

> At the corner of Fourth and Walnut [in Louisville, Kentucky], in the center of the shopping district, I was suddenly overwhelmed with the realization that I loved all those people, that they were mine and I theirs, that we could not be alien to one another even though we were total strangers. It was like waking from a dream of separateness, of spurious self-isolation in a special world, the world of renunciation and supposed holiness. The whole illusion of a separate holy existence is a dream.[62]

As Christopher Page points out, "Merton discovered that 'holiness' does not mean separateness. Holiness means a deeper awareness of connection."

I believe that non-dual experiences are more common than we think. This is borne out in a January 1976 *New York Times* magazine article on the phenomenon of non-dual experiences, which cited "a survey showing that at least 25 percent of the population has had at least one experience that they described as 'a sense of the unity of everything.'"[63] That was in 1976. The percentage has probably gone up by now. One woman told me that when she was walking along Long Beach on the west coast of Vancouver Island, she felt completely at one with the sand, sea, sky, sun, and every living thing. There was no separation. What joy!

If we look closely, we can literally see the unitive/non-dual in nature. The spiral seems to have unitive properties, and spirals are found all through nature, from the spiral galaxies of stars in unimaginable profusion throughout the universe to the spirals of life in our own DNA. The interior walls of my family's cabin on the west coast of Vancouver Island are panelled in knotty pine. The knots in the wood, sometimes spaced out but more often clumped together, look much like galaxies and clusters of galaxies. Surrounded on all sides in the bedroom by the knotty pine panelling, I have many times over the years lain in bed and seen giant elliptical galaxies, open-faced and edge-on spiral galaxies, and irregular galaxies. I am intrigued and fascinated by the fact that I can see a fairly realistic copy of the universe inside a tree, and that the universe appears to be mirrored in the vast outside as well as the deep inside of things. Metaphors can be misleading, but to me this speaks of a marvellous unity that is in everything and through everything. Who is to say that the universe isn't one giant tree with the galaxies as the "knots" or interiors of the limbs? It's a thought to have fun with!

The only unitive experience I have had occurred around the beginning of the millennium, and I still grapple to put some of it into words. The experience left a deep impression on me and I think of it often. I was in my local public library branch, standing near the computer terminals. There was a lot of quiet movement as everyone went about their business. Suddenly in this active silence I had a sense of every person and every thing completely infused with love. No one else had any sense that I was experiencing this, of course, as I watched people check books out or move about the library. I could sense with crystal clarity how precious and beloved everyone and everything was. There was no separation; everything functioned as a whole or as one. If one atom were removed from existence, it would be missed. I remember thinking that if a catastrophic earthquake happened at that moment and all was destroyed, everything would be fine because it was gently cradled in the eternal arms of God/Love. Of course it would have been nice to carry on in this state forever, but these states come to an end sooner than we would like. For one thing, when you really become aware of the state and begin to observe it, the experience changes, rather as an observer affects a quantum theory experiment. Secondly, the reality of my day crashed in on the state and I let it go because I had other things I needed to do.

I believe I was transformed by the wisdom I gained during the short time of this mystical experience. I have no idea why this experience came to me then except that perhaps at last, in my early forties, I was able to receive and recognize it. The main impression that has remained with me from this non-dual experience is that everything works as a whole and everything is infinitely precious, infinitely loved. I believe a non-dual experience is about the closest my finite human brain will come to comprehending the infinite Godhead.

Cynthia Bourgeault says of love, "The fact remains that love is a relational word . . . In order for love to manifest, there must first be duality."[64] So perhaps the real wonder of a non-dual experience is that, paradoxically, we are able to sense not only the dualistic but also the non-dualistic at the same time, and therefore we experience intense love as well as the oneness of everything. When we can hold the dual and the non-dual, we can dance at the still point. The dual and the non-dual become enfolded in each other.

Everything exists because of love. I believe this is why Jesus emphasized that we must "Love one another," because the more harmony there is in the whole, the more beautifully everything works together.

Imagine if we kept even the memory of a non-dual experience foremost in our hearts. I believe there would soon be peace on Earth, maybe no disease, no war, no one starving, and perhaps we would have the opportunity to fulfill our human potential. If ever during a non-dual experience someone were to give me a knowing look that said, "I am experiencing what you are experiencing," then I would know that I could get no closer to the kingdom of God.

Everything is loved in a way that is beyond our comprehension. What joy!

> All the particles of the world
> Are in love and looking for lovers.
> Pieces of straw tremble
> In the presence of amber.
>
> Rumi

It seems the whole of creation is quivering with love, as though it can hardly bear even the appearance of separateness.

Through investigations into quantum theory, science is beginning to give us a taste of a non-dual universe. In their book *Beyond Biocentrism*, Robert Lanza and Bob Berman write, "What it really means is that there is an underlying reality that connects all the universe's contents. In this place, no separations exist between anything and anything else. Yet this realm creates events that materialize in space-time, in the observable physical cosmos."[65]

To me, a mystical experience needs no understanding because it passes all understanding. Mysticism is at the heart and depth of all the great religions. All people experience the mystical in their lives, but we often don't recognize it. People may say, "You can go off the deep end with your inner imaginings." This is true, but if you know your inscape in any depth, your "gut" will tell you what should be regarded. Cynthia Bourgeault likens this to the sensitivity of experienced sailors who can gauge how close they are to land, even if they are in thick fog, by the look and smell of the wind and waves. We must use a sailor's intuition, as it were, to keep us on course.

Premonitions and Telepathy

Premonitions and telepathy seem closely related to me. The following story seems to be a mixture of both. I have had many experiences of premonition and telepathy in my life, but this one is more difficult to explain as anything other than premonition/telepathy.

One evening in my late teens I suddenly jumped up from the dinner table and said, "I've got to go babysitting." I rushed to check the calendar in my bedroom to see where I was to babysit. I soon came back to the table and said, "That's funny. I don't have anything written down on my calendar."

Just then the phone rang. The callers were people for whom I regularly babysat, and they asked, "Can you come and babysit?"

I asked, "When?" and they replied, "As soon as you can."

The odds are too great for this to be chance; not only did I anticipate that I was needed (premonition), I also perceived the exact thoughts of the people who needed me (telepathy). I need no more proof to know that we are most certainly connected at levels we are not aware of.

On other occasions I have heard and felt the thoughts of others in their own voices. I can think of three characteristics that were present in every case: the other person was telepathically gifted, their thought involved me, and there was a mutual attraction between us. I find it's easiest to hear or sense the thoughts of men to whom I'm attracted—which does not surprise me in the least. It makes sense that attraction assists this kind of communication! As I've mentioned previously, the more deeply we love people, the more accessible they are to us.

As is the case for all spiritual experiences, silence is the first necessary thing. There can be external noise going on, but one needs a profound inner silence or stillness for telepathic communication. From my experience, you do not have to be looking at the person; they can be a great distance away. In the case of the family that wanted me to babysit, they lived a couple of hundred meters away. At times I have connected with family members when we were on opposite sides of the world. Mediums will tell you this too.

From a scientific point of view, I have heard we are now at the point where we can discern the difference in brain waves between "yes" and "no". Every thought has its own energy; if you are sensitive to that energy, you know the thought. When I hear or sense a thought, I experience it just as the thinker does. This is similar to a unitive experience but not nearly as complete an experience.

There are dangers to telepathy. Although you know the other person's thoughts, you don't know why they are thinking them. You can end up jumping to conclusions which are not true or only partially true. As an example, I believed that one man whose thoughts I could sometimes read was seriously attracted to me, but it turned out to be a passing fancy. As you can imagine, this led to embarrassment on both our parts.

As well, psychical and mediumistic gifts are not necessarily a sign of spiritual maturity. We can exercise them even if we have not developed detachment and kenosis through inner work. This can be dangerous when the ego is in control, as the gifts could be used to control others, an abusive and damaging practice. Wisdom is needed to bring goodness from telepathy, just as it is needed for all gifts.

Many people have had the experience of thinking of someone, hearing the phone ring, and answering it, only to find the person they were thinking of on the other end, similar to my story above. Occasionally I have had the experience of thinking of something that happens a short while later. For example, I was stopped at a red light in a left-turn lane, and the thought came into my mind: "What if someone walked into my lane?" About a minute later, just as the green left-turn arrow came on for my lane, a man appeared in the crosswalk in front of me. The thought had prepared me so I was able to react quickly. If not, I might very well have hit him. I honked and he jumped a mile. He was totally oblivious to the fact that the light had turned green for the cars.

Some people believe that our lives are happening all at once, but our finite minds can only comprehend them in a linear fashion. Perhaps premonitions are proof that "All time is eternally present,"[66] and that we have access to the eternal present. When we are able to see from a higher level, we will have a much more complete and non-dual view of things. If we were able to see some of the things coming in our lives, we might get out of the way more often!

A Visit to the Psychic-Medium

In July 1976, when I was seventeen years old, I saw an English psychic named Les Dukes on a local TV program. The way he talked about God impressed me, and each person who phoned in to speak with him seemed happy with the reading they received. For a number of years I had experienced headaches and other symptoms, and no one seemed to know what the cause was. I thought it would be interesting to schedule a reading with Mr. Dukes, although my mother was not happy about the idea.

I was very nervous as the session started. Les Dukes was a middle-aged man with a Cockney accent. He told a few jokes to try to put me at my ease, which unfortunately didn't help me relax. He said he had no crystal ball and that nothing was hidden under the carpet; he obviously felt my skepticism and apprehension.

He began by saying that there was no time in the spirit world.

I asked, "What do you mean?"

He was a bit impatient with my question and just repeated that there was no time in the spirit world, and that he might tell me things from my past, my present, or my future. (I was so tied to time at that stage of my life that a world without time seemed inconceivable. Now I can be at home in an eternal world.)

He asked me not to fold my arms over my chest (I presume this blocked energy) and to keep talking. He obviously sensed energy from the main part of my body and also got cues from my speaking voice.

The first thing he asked me was "Why didn't your mother come?"

I had asked my mother to come with me, but she didn't want to—she didn't even want me to go for a reading. At the last minute she changed her mind, but I dug my heels in and said, "No, it's O.K." I felt if she hadn't supported me at the beginning, I didn't want her to come. A few years later I realized he probably wished to speak to her about her future heart problems.

When Mr. Dukes first began to read me—or perhaps "make contact with me" is a better way of putting it—I sensed my mind expand. Or was it his mind that expanded? It was hard to tell. I also felt more emotional.

He said, "I know what you have come here for today so don't tell me. There's a ring for you. Not a wedding ring. I don't see that for a few years. [I am still waiting for that to come to pass.] You're not wearing the ring. Why not?"

I was confused. The only ring I could think of was a family ring that was set with diamonds. I said, "Because it's too expensive."

He passed on to the reason I had come to see him. He said, "Not that long ago, when you were seven or eight, you had a blow to your head."

I was knocked sideways (appropriate description!) by this statement because I suddenly remembered getting what was probably a concussion when I was hit in the head by a baseball bat during a game of baseball unsupervised by adults. All I could say was an amazed "Yes!"

"Was it on the left side of my head?" I asked. I'm not sure why I asked this question, but I think I had forgotten and was confused as to which side was hit.

He replied, "No, not the left side, the right side. That is important."[67] Then he added, "It is nothing serious, don't worry about it. The symptoms are about as bad as they are going to get."

He moved on. "I get a good feeling about music. Oh yes, you're good at it," and he gave a snort, as if to say that was a no-brainer.

At this my skepticism was dispelled. A couple of days earlier, while playing the piano and pondering the upcoming visit, I thought, "I wonder if he will say I am good at music?" That question was obviously psychically still around me.

Staying on the subject of music, he said, "Yes, that will fit in rather well."

This statement intrigued me and helped propel me toward a career in music. At the age of seventeen, anything seemed possible. I think I had big ideas that I might become famous. My musical career turned out to be something far more mundane, but in some ways it worked out well given the course my life and health have taken.

At some point during the reading I told him I had had a mystical experience (I am sure I did not use the word "mystical," but something like it), and he told me, "You will get it again."

He asked me why I kept thinking I was going to die. He also named three tendencies of mine: that I could be fiery and impatient, and that I worried, worried, worried. It would have been nice if he had named three positive characteristics as well. However, I know that through inner work and transformation these negative tendencies are less severe than they once were.

Toward the end of the reading I asked how my sister was. He said she was fine and would continue to be fine. I asked about her state six months earlier. Mr. Dukes said, "I don't like that at all." Which was correct, as at that time she had been having headaches so severe they caused her to pass out a couple of times. The doctors couldn't figure out why. However, once she had her wisdom teeth removed, the terrible headaches ceased and she was fine.

A couple of days later I went to see my friend Margot Galloway, a woman of my mum's generation, and told her of this extraordinary visit to Mr. Dukes. She said he sounded like the real thing, not a fake. As I was giving her a blow-by-blow account of the reading, I mentioned that he had said there was a ring for me.

She said, "Just a minute. I have a ring for you," and went into her house. When she returned, she brought a ring with three stones in it—two agates on either side of a garnet. "This is for you," she said. "I got it from my Auntie May, who got it from her aunt. They both had psychic and healing abilities."

I said, "Shouldn't it go to your daughter?"

Margot said, "It doesn't necessarily work that way." She handed it to me and then continued, "You can do what you like with it, make it bigger or smaller. Whatever happens to it is meant to happen to it. It will get to whoever it needs to get to."

I was excited and flabbergasted by this revelation.

She told me a story of going to a medium when she was younger. A friend had health problems and wanted to know what the medium would say. Margot accompanied her friend to provide support. The medium said to Margot, "You are so close to the spirit world you are almost healing her."

So what is the meaning of the ring? Margot said it is just a small thing, but I think it is the sign of a line of women who have a gift. I assume that sometime in the future I will, perhaps under interesting circumstances, pass the ring on to a young woman to carry on the work.

About six months later, Mr. Dukes was invited to speak at my high school. I was not pleased to see him. By this time, many of the ramifications of the reading had dawned in my conscious mind. My life was not going to be the happy, relatively easy existence I had hoped for. This had sent me into a depression that lasted for three or four years. I also felt he had wrenched some information out of me, and this made me angry. I had been exposed to things I was not ready to be exposed to, and this can have negative consequences. So the reading had some positive aspects, but there were dangers too.

At times during the session I felt he was talking above my understanding, but now much of what he said is clear to me. It is very curious to experience what you later realize is someone talking to a future self that has not yet come into being.

Dreams: Out of Waking Hours

> Our heart oft-times wakes when we sleep, and God
> can speak to that, either by words, by proverbs, by
> signs and similitudes, as well as if one was awake.
>
> John Bunyan, *The Pilgrim's Progress*

Occasionally I have felt as though, overnight, I have grown
spiritually. When I wake up in the morning I feel something has
widened or opened, or I understand things better. I also notice
I am far more creative in my dreams than during waking hours.
In some dreams I seem to be a gifted interior decorator, which
is something I know little about in waking consciousness.

When I awake, sometimes I remember things I did and said,
often long forgotten, which I feel very remorseful about. When
this happens, I assume that my subconscious has brought the
memories to the surface to be forgiven and healed. As many of
us have experienced, in our sleep we may visit realms that we
are unaware of, or only vaguely aware of, in our waking hours.
This experience is beautifully expressed in Antonio Machado's
poem "Last Night."

> Last night, as I was sleeping,
> I dreamt—marvelous error!—
> that a spring was breaking
> out in my heart.
> I said: Along which secret aqueduct,
> oh water, are you coming to me,
> water of a new life
> that I have never drunk?
>
> Last night, as I was sleeping,
> I dreamt—marvelous error!—
> that I had a beehive
> here inside my heart.

And the golden bees
were making white combs
and sweet honey
from my old failures.

Last night, as I was sleeping,
I dreamt—marvelous error!—
that a fiery sun was giving light inside my heart.
It was fiery because I felt
warmth as from a hearth,
and sun because it gave light
and brought tears to my eyes.

Last night, as I slept,
I dreamt—marvelous error!—
that it was God I had
here inside my heart.[68]

I once had a dream where I sensed someone who had died ten years previously was asking forgiveness for things she had said thirty years earlier. I do remember being annoyed and hurt at the time by some of the things she had said, but until the dream I had honestly forgotten her words. I believe that not only was she being purified, but I was also being purified, as I had held those things against her for thirty years without realizing it. The golden bees were indeed making white combs and sweet honey from our old failures.

By far the most amazing and vivid experience I have had with dreams was a communication from my maternal grandfather. One night between Christmas 1991 and New Year's Day 1992 I had a dream unlike any I have had before or since. Out of a billowing cloud of light appeared a face that shone with light (I know it sounds melodramatic, but it really was that way). It was the face of my maternal grandfather. Although he had died thirty-one years before I was born, I knew his face well from photographs. I was anxious for a message and tried to grab at it rather than let it come, so all I got from him was something like "I love you all very much."

In the morning I awoke, remembered the vivid dream, and became rather worried. I thought, "I think this means either something very good or something very bad will happen. I think it is probably something very bad." Within the next couple of weeks the whole family planned to go to Mexico to visit my sister, who was living there at the time. I was concerned that the dream might be an omen that something unfortunate was going to happen to us on the trip. We went to Mexico and had a safe trip and a wonderful time. But the dream remained uneasily in the back of my mind.

Near the beginning of April, I awoke during the night to hear Mum saying something to Dad about her nitroglycerin pills. At that moment I knew what the dream was about. There followed an extremely stressful time in our lives. Within a month Mum had her second open heart surgery. Right after the operation it was touch and go whether she would pull through. Since my sister was still working in Mexico, much of the burden of the situation fell on me. Not surprisingly, the stress exacerbated my Sjogren syndrome, always an unpleasant experience. However, the dream turned out to be the greatest gift my grandfather could have given me, providing me with strength and comfort many times during the ordeal. It was a great comfort to know that loved ones in other realms were ready to help during difficult times.

An interesting footnote to the dream: Several years later I related this story to Bruno Barnhart, a Camoldolese monk. He insightfully said, "You had a transfiguration experience followed by a time of trial."

I think we are more connected to one another during our dreams than we realize. I have had dreams where I found myself discussing my values and opinions. I believe this is part of what

I call deep background work. There is a lot more of this type of work going on in the world than we suppose, and I believe it stimulates a good deal of the change in world consciousness.

We Saw Him Before He Left . . .

> The deepest part of our being comes from beyond time.
>
> Cynthia Bourgeault

> Where did you come from, baby dear?
> Out of the everywhere into the here.
>
> George MacDonald

One day while babysitting my nephew Jeremy, then about eighteen months old, a very intense thought came into my mind. He was so adorably cute and cuddly, I was sorry that my grandparents, long gone from this world, weren't here to see or experience him. As I climbed the stairs with my nephew, I was thinking intensely of them and thought, "He is so adorable, I wish you could see him."

Immediately I heard a reply in my head: "We saw him before he left."

Not only did I not expect a reply, but the content of the reply was something I could not have anticipated, so while it came from within me, I know it didn't come from me. I strongly believe this experience was genuine, mainly because it was so unexpected and immediate.

When I think about the reply, it opens up a can of philosophical and spiritual worms. The reply suggests that we exist before we come into our bodies—i.e., we are eternal beings—that there are obviously "family" meetings in the world of the spirit, that spiritual connections between the living and the dead are stronger than we think . . .

It also raises questions: What do we say to one another before we leave? Do we get assignments before we come to earth? How come we can't remember our previous state before this existence? Do we know the general shape our lives will take? Perhaps we do know, since at this stage we are in the eternal, where time does not exist as we know it on earth.

Unexpected replies are great, but they do leave you with more questions!

For me, this experience underlines the quote, "We are not human beings having a spiritual experience but spiritual beings having a human experience."

Synchronicity

The recognition of any mystical experience is, I think, a fruit of surrender.[69] Synchronicity, "meaningful patterns of coincidence," which I mentioned in the chapter "Suffering and Inner Transformation," is another form of mystical experience. One of the more mystical synchronous experiences I have had took place during a five-day wisdom school retreat on Saltspring Island. It was a Monday-to-Friday retreat, and the middle day, Wednesday, was the one day of complete silence. We had a three-hour break after lunch. I was staying with Yvonne, so I drove back from the retreat location with her. A third retreatant, Judy (of the crying child story), was in the car as well. As we drove, Yvonne played a CD of monks chanting. The chanting was wonderful, powerful, and filled the car with a profound atmosphere.

At the bottom of a hill, just before the road turned a corner, we saw a boy standing at the roadside holding two pieces of driftwood so that they formed a cross. Because of the rule of silence, none of us spoke at the time, but we found later that we were all having similar thoughts of surprise and amazement. There was no reason for this boy of about nine to hold two pieces of wood so that they formed a cross. There was no accident around the corner or any reason to slow down. What was he doing? The glorious chanting and the unexpected cross came together to create an unforgettable mystical experience. Judy later said it was as if the world turned upside down for a moment.

The American writer Gail Godwin writes of a story of the heart she is reminded of through a daily routine she has adopted.

> Filling the vase has become part of my morning rhythm. Even in the depth of winter I give myself the present of plopping in fresh water something that has grown out of the earth, a sprig of white pine or hemlock, red berries and thorns, and setting it on the sill beside the computer. Now it is pansy and nasturtium time again, and when I pick the first nasturtiums I always remember a story my literary agent told me.
>
> His mother, Mrs. Hawkins, grew nasturtiums all winter in her greenhouse; they clambered all winter, orange and salmon and golden yellow, up their indoor trellises. One cold winter night, she and her husband were on the way to their chamber orchestra rehearsal. They were too early, so they decided to take a detour to look at a new building along the road down by the river. Suddenly the headlights of their car shone on an older woman, whom they knew slightly, walking beside the river. As it was so cold, they stopped and offered her a ride home. She accepted. When they let her off at her house, Mrs. Hawkins gave her the jar of nasturtiums she had picked to give "to someone or other" at the rehearsal.
>
> A few weeks later the Hawkinses received a note from the woman saying she had been depressed all winter and was on her way to drown herself in the river. But when they suddenly stopped and

offered her a ride and gave her those bright summer flowers in the depth of winter, she took it as a sign from God that she was supposed to go on living.

A woman whose life was saved by a bouquet of nasturtiums. But someone's heart had to be tuned in to the rhythms that count; Marian Hawkins had to understand the value of growing nasturtiums in the wintertime in order for there to *be* such bouquets to give to "someone or other" in need of a reminder of summer. She and her husband had to be the sort of people who were curious enough about something new to go out of their way to see how it was coming along, the sort of people who without thinking twice would divert their point-to-point journey a second time to run a solitary woman home on a cold night. Heart acts are often improvisational detours from point-to-point plans.[70]

In the second sentence of the last paragraph, "tuned in to the rhythms that count" is a wonderful phrase. In a word it says to me "synchronicity." When we are in synchronicity, we act from upwelling depths, "the root of the root of ourselves" as Rumi puts it. Notice the inner work that has taken place. These people let go of their own agenda, and Mrs. Hawkins, I am sure, at a deep level, sensed the older woman's depression and despair. She became compassion absolute. When we are present like this, we become perfect vessels for the divine—angels unawares.

I am sure most of us can think of times when we experienced synchronicities, incredible gifts from God. Several years ago I sat on a park bench the day before Mother's Day. I was feeling very sad and sorry for myself, yet again, that I was not a mother. A little girl came running over to me with a beautiful rhododendron blossom. She said, "Here, this is for you." I managed to thank her before she ran away to her father. For me, my thoughts and the beautiful action of the little girl ran together. I felt God was comforting me in a very lovely way. An example of synchronicity—a gift from God. It was a very small act done with great love, as Mother Teresa would say, that had far-reaching healing. The young girl, without recognizing it on the surface, was "tuned in to the rhythms that count."

Shortly after I started to write this book, I experienced another instance of synchronicity. I had been writing on my parents' computer, at their house, but I reached a point where I felt I needed a computer at my own home so I could work on the book at any time. For several months I wondered how I could afford even a second-hand computer on my tight budget. One Sunday after a tiring and stressful Saturday, I decided I needed a quiet "cocoon day." I skipped church and rested up. After a while I noticed a garage sale taking place at the condo building next door. I thought I would pop across as I was looking for a large sun umbrella. I had completely forgotten about my search for a computer. I didn't find the umbrella, but I did come across an old laptop, ideal for my word-processing needs. The price was only fifty dollars—still a squeeze on my budget, but I managed. Occasionally it pays to miss church!

Places and Atmospheres

Sensitive people often talk of the "atmosphere" of places. I have experienced places where the feeling was unpleasant or uncomfortable, and others where the feeling has been very peaceful and even happy. That spiritual imprints are left in places is well known, and silence allows people to sense these imprints.

A couple of places with unpleasant, uncomfortable feelings come to mind. One is Mitla in the state of Oaxaca, Mexico. The name Mitla came to Spanish from Mictlan, which means "place of the dead" or "underworld" in the Nahuatl language. This was a major religious centre and burial place for the Zapotecs. We visited there as a family in 1992, and we were, unusually for us, crabby with each other, as though there were something oppressive that we couldn't shake. Then Mum hit her head on the beam of a low door; our concern for her overcame whatever had possessed us and we fortunately snapped out of our foul mood. Several years later I was reading a blog by someone who had visited Mitla and had a similar experience. He felt a sense of menace. I absolutely would not stop anyone going to Mitla—it is an interesting and beautiful archeological site, well worth a visit, and I am sure most people who go there don't sense anything and have a good time, but it doesn't hurt to provide this warning.

On the other hand, there are places that have peaceful, healing atmospheres. One such place was the chapel at the Prince of Peace Priory in Chemainus, BC. As soon as I walked into this beautiful little chapel, panelled in redwood, I felt engulfed by a profound silence and peace. Other people sensed the very same thing about the chapel. Sadly, this sacred space was later dismantled and the property sold.

Sensing the atmosphere around us is a type of inner awakening. Let us make places of healing and peace.

SENSES OF ANOTHER REALITY

> . . . a far green country opened before him under a
> swift sunrise.

> Frodo's first glimpse of the undying lands in *The Lord
> of the Rings: The Return of the King* by J.R.R. Tolkien

The spiritual journey of our lives can be seen as a migration from the outside to the inside. If we practise spiritual awakeness, then as we mature we become more aware and connected to the subtleties of our inner life. When we physically die, it can be said in every sense that we go from the outside to the inside. This idea is echoed by out-of-body experiencer Jurgen Ziewe, "When the relay station and filter, which is our brain, stops functioning and the body is returned to its individual atoms, our conscious and subconscious mind become our new external reality."[71]

We usually perceive others, and the universe, through our senses of sight, hearing, touch, taste, and smell. However, when a person dies we perceive them through memory and our inner senses, which come from a different realm beyond the physical. Just as scientific instruments—telescopes and microscopes, for example—can be intensifiers for our external senses, love is an intensifier for our internal senses. The more deeply we love someone, the more accessible they are to us in the interior realms.

This was well summed up by Hugo Dyson when he spoke at the funeral of Charles Williams, one of his fellow Inklings (a group of mostly Oxford dons).

> It is not blasphemous to believe that what was true of Our Lord is, in its less degree, true of all who are in Him. They go away in order to be with us in a new way, even closer than before. A month ago I would have called this silly sentiment. Now I know better. He seems, in some indefinable way, to be all around us now. I do not doubt he is doing and will do for us all sorts of things he could not have done while in the body.[72]

Likewise, St. Dominic said, "Do not weep, for I shall be more useful to you after my death and I shall help you then more effectively than during my life." I sense this is true because I believe we continue to grow after death, and therefore become even more potent for good than we were in life. This view is especially comforting to those with disabilities, promising that we will be able to do things for others that we could not do while in our bodies. Even healthy, energetic people who are spiritually awake feel frustrated that they cannot do more for others. Therefore, Henri Nouwen's words are of great comfort:

> You and I have to trust that our short little lives can bear fruit far beyond the boundaries of our chronologies. But we have to choose this and trust deeply that we have a spirit to send that will bring joy, peace and life to those who will remember us. Francis of Assisi died in 1226, but he is still very much alive! His death was a true gift. And today, nearly eight centuries later, he continues to fill his brothers and sisters, within and without the Franciscan orders, with great energy and life. He died but never died. His life goes on bearing new

fruit around the world. His spirit keeps descending upon us. More than ever I am convinced that death can, indeed, be chosen as our final gift of life.[73]

I have felt many times that loved ones who have died were closer and more accessible to me than when they were in the body. They may be out of sight but not out of mind—or heart.

Sir Walter Scott said, "Is death the last step? No, it is the final awakening." I have heard death called the final healing. I truly believe that nothing in physical death is final, but it is only a continuation of the eternal consciousness.

> Life is eternal; love is immortal; and death is only a horizon; and a horizon is nothing save the limit of our sight.
>
> Rossiter Worthington Raymond (1840–1918)

Here are some final words from well-known people that I have found interesting and encouraging:

> It is very beautiful over there.
>
> Thomas Edison

> This isn't bad. Tell everyone this really isn't bad at all . . . it's beautiful out there!
>
> Stephen Foster

> Is this dying? Is this all? Is this what I feared when I prayed against a hard death? Oh, I can bear this! I can bear it!
>
> Cotton Mather

OH WOW, OH WOW, OH WOW.

> Steve Jobs

For humour, I have to add Oscar Wilde's last words. Seeing the ugly wallpaper of the room in which he was dying, he remarked, "Well—one of us has to go."[74]

When these deathbed comments are put together with Jesus's beautiful words on the next life—"Today you will be with me in paradise" (Luke 23:43)—the evidence is overwhelming for the continuation of the spirit in eternal life. Still, with all this evidence, and the evidence of my own experience with loved ones who have gone on, there are, I must admit, occasional times (it grows less with age!) when I am still anxious about death.

I agree with John Polkinghorne's views of the world of the spirit:

> People sometimes say that they would certainly like more life than this world affords, but not a life that goes on without an end. They fear eventual boredom . . . If our future life depended upon our own finite resources, these fears would be justified. But the quality of the life of the world to come depends upon the limitless resources of God, and so it will prove to be a life of unending fulfillment.[75]

and

> If there will turn out to be those who will resist that love for ever, with its offer of forgiveness and redemption, then they will have condemned themselves to live the life of hell. They will not be in a place of torment, painted red, but in a place of infinite boredom, painted grey, from which the divine life has deliberately been excluded by the choice of its inhabitants. The best imaginative picture that I know of hell is not the torture chambers of Dante's *Inferno,* but the dreary town,

lost down a crack in the floor of heaven, of C.S. Lewis's *The Great Divorce*.[76]

Accounts I have read by mediums or by those people who have had near-death or out-of-body experiences indicate that both places exist. For example, in *The Wheel of Eternity*, author and medium Helen Greaves writes that "The Mistress" while on earth was rich, beautiful, selfish, hated her husband, was mean to her servants, and despised her mentally challenged son. She found herself after death in a dirty hovel surrounded by unkind people. Her mentally challenged son on the other hand was an advanced soul and after death found himself in a beautiful place of love and light.[77] Occasionally mediums and out of body experiencers have reported not only dark, dreary lands filled with people who torment each other but some report burning bodies.[78]

I like Henri Nouwen's words of wisdom on the subject of death:

> All that our society has to say suggests that death is the great enemy who will finally get the better of us against our will and desire. But thus perceived, life is little more than a losing battle, a hopeless struggle, a journey of despair. My own vision and yours too, I hope, is radically different. Even though I often give in to the many fears and warnings of my world, I still believe deeply that our few years on this earth are part of a much larger event that stretches out far beyond the boundaries of our birth and death. I think of it as a mission into time, a mission that is very exhilarating and even exciting, mostly because the One who sent me on the mission is waiting for me to come home and tell the story of what I have learned.[79]

We must be able to die to ourselves and take the kenotic, self-emptying journey, just as Jesus did, to see and be part of the larger event.

I believe I have received a few communications from loved ones who have gone on to the realm of pure consciousness. These communications are known as After Death Communications (ADCs). The following five sections as well as the "*We saw him before he left*" section are examples of ADCs I have experienced.

Jenny

My friend Jenny had a difficult life in the physical world. At about the age of eleven she went into kidney failure, and from then on she was often in hospital for surgery or regulation. She had two kidney transplants, neither of which worked for any length of time, and two hip replacements because medications had eaten away her joints. She also had part of her intestines removed. Along the way she developed diabetes and went blind. Finally, at age thirty-seven, her heart simply stopped.

Although her death was not unexpected, it was still a great loss for all who knew her. I remember her as an exceptionally cheerful person despite all her afflictions, and she was very helpful to me because she had already been on the "living with a disability path" for some years before I joined her. She had a *great* sense of humour, and we had many good laughs together. Her packed memorial service was a wonderful tribute to her, full of laughter and good memories.

About eighteen months after her death, I had a communication from her. She told me that she no longer needed "*the prayer.*" At first I did not understand what she was talking about, but then I remembered that I had had a prayer for her when she was alive: I would ask that if God was to heal anyone, it would be her. I never told her about this prayer, but she certainly knew about it now.

This statement simply highlights the fact that we are much more aware of others' thoughts and prayers in the eternal realm. A second thing this communication pointed out was that Jenny must indeed be feeling very good about things if she did not feel in need of prayer. She would not have turned down prayers for herself in this life. I *know* the body she has now causes her no trouble at all.

Even after this communication from Jenny, I still worried about her life, felt sorry for her, and felt the unfairness of her life. A couple of years after that first communication, I sensed another communication from her. She told me to stop fussing about her life. I knew the communication had to be from Jenny because she disliked people fussing about her. Everyone who knew her can still probably hear her saying "Yeah, yeah, yeah . . ." which she did if someone fussed over her. I sensed she now did not feel her life was unfair. As I mentioned in the "Inner Universe" chapter, unfairness seems to permeate the physical realm, but perhaps this communication from Jenny indicates that, in the larger view, disability and unfairness, as well as death, lose their sting. When we know we are deeply loved and are now happy, how can unfairness wound us?

A few years after her death, Jenny's parents placed a bench in her memory along a favourite walk of hers in the Songhees neighbourhood overlooking Victoria's Inner Harbour. A plaque on the bench is inscribed with her name, dates, and the question "Have you hugged your kidney today?" It is so typical of Jenny's sense of humour, and it reminds us all to give thanks for the health we do have.

Peter

I had known Peter, the father of one of my best friends, since I was two. Peter was a respected family physician and a man of many talents and interests. He lived a full life and died at the age of seventy-seven from cancer. About three months after he died, I believe I received a communication from him. He told me that he didn't realize what a tough time I was having. I was moved to tears by this communication, which again proved to me that in the next life we are much more aware of others' conditions. If we strove in this life to be sensitive to the needs and conditions of our fellow human beings, our awareness would bring a bit of heaven to Earth. When he was still with us on this planet, I told Peter about the caring I received when I went to a Reiki treatment, and he said he wished he could spend that quality, caring time with his patients. Currently doctors rarely have that kind of time to spend with their patients, but I have a suspicion Peter is able to do that now.

Dorothy

Dorothy was my neighbour for a couple of years before she died of cancer at the age of ninety. She had an unusually sharp mind, a good sense of humor, and was a faithful member of our centering prayer group. A few months after she died I had a very clear communication from her. She told me she had had an easy transition to the next life, which I was very glad to hear.

I had always wanted to do more travelling when I inherited a bit of money, but I was also concerned about my health, so I thought maybe I would put off travelling until the next life. The clear message I got from Dorothy was that I should travel now, in this life, if I could. I took her advice and am very glad I did. I have seen some beautiful parts of the world, and with careful planning it has not been too harmful to my health.

Mum

How do you write about your mother? Mum died, not unexpectedly but very suddenly, in April 2008. She was such a vibrant person—people said they couldn't believe she had gone. She was a person of deep faith, and she lived her faith. People said she was also one of the most positive people they had ever known. So many have said they miss her smiling face and zest for life. She was the heart of our family, so her leaving left a large hole.

Since she has gone, I have sensed her many times. About three weeks after she died I had a dream where I found myself really wanting to know how she was getting on. In the dream I heard her say, "I'm not just happy, I'm very happy." I hold on to that thought.

A few weeks later I thought of Mum while I was out for a walk. At that moment on the road I saw a happy face made by the shadows of leaves on a tree. The "eyes" twinkled in the breeze. I like to think it was Mum smiling at me!

I have had dreams in which we just spent time together, but nearly two years after she died I believe I had rather a special dream in which she tried to heal me. For a short while during the dream I sensed I had no pain or inflammation in my body. What joy! This gives me hope that Sjogren syndrome can be overcome.

I have sensed that her death was not only a release for her, but has also released me in some ways. Mum has become finer? Subtler? More purified? I'm not sure how to describe it, but I seem to get only as much of her as I want. Overbearing is not the right word to use when speaking of Mum, but she had a strong presence, and this presence does not overshadow me anymore.

About six years after she died I had an important decision to make. I asked her what I should do. Frustratingly, I simply received silence. This is probably because there seems to be a "prime directive" of non-interference in other people's lives. I went back and forth, back and forth with the issue, unable to decide until the last minute. As soon as I made the decision I heard a huge interior sigh—I guess I had made the right choice! But it wasn't until about eighteen months later that I realized why it had been right, simply because if I had chosen the other route, it would have made the situation much more difficult.

Mum had such a strong faith. One of her best friends, Barb, asked her, "Mary, what do you think the next world is like?"

She replied, "I don't know what it is like, but because God made it, it will be good."

Dad

My father died in December 2014 at the age of 104. He led a remarkable life. He was a strong and healthy man, and he was perhaps never happier than when he was walking in nature. He adored God's creation.

Dad was blessed to die peacefully in his sleep. I received a phone call from my brother, telling me of our father's death, shortly after midnight on December 21. After the phone call I sat in bed, unable to sleep as my mind was completely filled with thoughts and memories of him. As I sat up in bed, I saw nothing but felt the firm pressure of fingertips pressing on my sternum. That I saw nothing suggests that Dad's energy was beyond the electromagnetic wavelength visible to my physical sight, but as I could feel his touch, our electrical fields were obviously still encountering each other.[80] I am glad I did not see anything, as I probably would have screamed and jumped out of bed, or become so emotional that I would have burst into tears. I am certain the touch was my father trying to indicate that he had made it to the other side and was fine.

It was a comfort to know that he was completely conscious so soon after death, and he was already aware that he had left this world. From what I have read about death and dying, I know that some people who fall asleep in this world, die in their sleep, and wake up in the "houses of healing" don't even realize they have died. Although Dad had died in his sleep, something or someone told him he was not dreaming, that he had died. I sense he had a guide with him. I even sense that he and the guide were on the left side of my bed. It would be just like my father to say to his guide, "I have to let her know that I am OK, that I have 'died' and have reached the other side." It is a relief to know that he was fully conscious of what was happening and that the "transition" had gone smoothly.

In May 2015 I had a dream that Dad was going through an investiture or initiation. In the dream he received something like a knighthood. It seems he had made rapid progress.

COMMUNITY

J ust as silence and contemplative prayer are essential for spiritual growth and transformation, community is also essential. A healthy community provides a loving environment that fosters growth, healing, and balance; helps to keep us on a healthy spiritual track; and encourages us on our spiritual journey. We are to "bear one another's burdens" (Galatians 6:2), and this, of course, needs to be done in community. Without a loving community, it is possible to go down dangerous paths, or become arrogant, thinking that we have no need of others' help.

I find I am most likely to go awry in a community when I spend time worrying about what other people are thinking or doing. When I do this, I am back in egoic consciousness. I think I am at last learning that the way I can most help my community is by doing my inner journey, so when the community calls upon me, I may have the inner wisdom to be of use. If we do not use inner wisdom, but simply work from our motivations, we risk being busybodies.

When there is spiritual health and depth in a community, amazing things happen. People can be the essence of God and know what we need before we ask (Matthew 6:8). And at unexpected times the profound depths can be revealed, exposing the glory of the kingdom of heaven!

In my experience, churches sometimes get caught up in what I call "superficial nice, nice." Years ago I remember a fellow parishioner saying, "Yes, but do we really *know* each other?" Really *knowing* each other takes honesty. This, in turn, takes trust, which requires that we are able to heal the ego and let go. This may not happen as often as it should in communities, although it is happening more and more as spiritual consciousness evolves.

If you wish to see communities with spiritual health and depth, seek out the professionals. *Into Great Silence* is an excellent documentary about a year in the life of a Trappist monastery in France. The brothers don't speak much or often, but when they do it is out of profound wisdom. As I listened to one monk talk, I felt like a spiritual dilettante. If church communities had more of these profound spiritual qualities, I am sure there would be fewer congregations shrinking and dying. Organizations like the Contemplative Society offer bridges between professional and non-professional worlds.

St. Benedict hit on one of the best formulas for community building and strengthening: *Ora et labora*—prayer and work. I was once part of a church community that built a new church. The lighter labour was done by the members, and we got to know each other in ways that we could not have foreseen. Some members of my present church community go to another church once a week and prepare lunch for the poor. This work has enormously strengthened community, not only for the hungry but also for those who work in the kitchen, where joy and laughter are the spiritual food. As has been noted earlier, praying together as a community connects us to one another in ways we cannot imagine. When we add communal work as well, it becomes an unrivalled combination.

Another kind of community connection took place during a retreat led by Lynn Baumann. Lynn was giving a fascinating presentation on metaphysics and hyper-dimensionality after lunch—perhaps not the best time to discuss weighty issues. He was making statements such as "Hyper-dimensional space vibrates on this plane and opens our heart" and "Scientific tradition says yes, hyper-dimensionality exists, but we don't quite know what to do with it. Sacred tradition says yes, hyper-dimensionality exists and we have access to it."[81]

I and others sensed the whole group was becoming physically weighed down by this intense intellectual and psychic download (Cynthia Bourgeault would call it vertical download). The weighty metaphysical discourse had a soporific effect. All I wanted to do was lie down and go to sleep. In fact, several times I felt myself listing to one side and had to pull myself upright so I didn't fall into the lap of my neighbour.

After a while, however, the group collectively seemed to take a big breath, and our energy was restored. It seems we had digested the weighty metaphysics (and our lunch!). This is the only time I can recall the download of information about another dimension/realm having a physical effect on a group of people. It is powerful stuff.

As we have learned, small interior changes can bring big changes in the exterior world. Gene Miller, an urban planner in Victoria, wrote about the Urban Development Institute's efforts to tackle the plight of homeless people in a fresh light. Members were encouraged to "think outside the box about the box" rather than treading the old paths of thinking. The group struggled with the problem, and "ideas, some of them innovative, did spill onto the table," but things did not really change until a perceptual change happened.

> Someone suggested: "What if, instead of talking about 'homelessness' or 'the homeless,' we talk about '*our* homeless'?" Immediately, the energy, the weather, in the room changed. Instinctively, folks knew that this was potentially a profound shift— one that could release entirely new approaches and responses.[82]

It is interesting to note that the barrier dissolved as soon as a non-dual approach was taken—the use of the word "our"—and a flood of energy and ideas was released. The group now knew it would be able to move forward and find more housing. This is one small instance of a shift from ordinary (egoic) to spiritual (non-dual/unitive) consciousness.

I must say a word about government. Some say that the government should have as little involvement as possible in people's lives. I don't agree. I think this makes the government the enemy, when in fact government should be our conscience. Good government's first priority must be to help the most vulnerable in any part of creation.

I am sure that our communities frequently, without even knowing it, tap into pools of wisdom that are like gusher oil wells. Wisdom teachers believe real wisdom lies in what is called "the conscious circle of humanity" or the communion of saints. "It consists of people, some in bodies, some beyond, who guide, give course corrections, provide wisdom to this beloved planet."[83] I remember hearing Lynn Bauman remark, during a spiritual practice workshop, "Who is to say that a group of fourteenth-century French nuns did not give us this space today." Similarly, I believe we provide spiritual space for those in the near and far future by creating spiritual space in the here and now. I love this kind of thought because of its grand expansiveness, its *metanoia* (big mind) as it is known in contemplative circles. Likewise, I know that we can help those who are struggling on "the other side" by praying and doing inner work. I agree with those who say this is a great work.

And *everyone* in a community can have profound wisdom to impart. In this success-driven world, intellectually challenged people are often overlooked and ignored. Nathan Ball is the former executive director of L'Arche Canada, the great work started by Jean Vanier, which establishes homes, programs, and support networks for people with developmental disabilities.

Nathan relates a story about Doug, a L'Arche member with an intellectual disability, and Katharina, one of the L'Arche assistants, who were on their way to do some shopping.

> As they were walking to the mall, they needed to pass by a bench on which three homeless men were sitting. Most people were either choosing to walk to the mall on a path that didn't involve passing this bench, or walking on the opposite edge of the path, avoiding all eye contact with the three homeless men. If it had been up to Katharina, they would have probably done the same thing.
>
> But that wasn't what Doug wanted to do!
>
> He walked right up to the three homeless men, said hello to each one of them and gave them all a high-five before continuing along the path.
>
> No money was exchanged. No "help" was given or offered. All that happened was simple human contact freely and joyfully given. "All" that happened was that five people—Doug, Katharina, and the three homeless men—felt better and more alive after the high-fives were given than they did before.[84]

When Doug saw the three homeless men, he came from a profound, non-judgmental place and look what happened! We need more of this type of being in our communities. I know I need to be more like Doug.

Doug shows us what being non-judgmental is all about. Just like a pearl of wisdom I heard on a recording of a Cynthia Bourgeault retreat. One of the retreatants said, "Enlightenment isn't about judgment and it isn't about other people." I am finding this statement takes a lifetime to learn.

I have heard the following story several times, used as an example of what a faith community needs to be like.

The Messiah Is One of You
Once upon a time there was an abbot of a monastery who was very good friends with the rabbi of a local synagogue. It was Europe, and times were hard. Sometimes the rabbi would come and pour out his soul to the abbot and the abbot would encourage him; other times the abbot would visit his friend the rabbi and pour out his difficulties and be comforted by the rabbi.

The abbot found his community dwindling and the faith life of his monks shallow and lifeless. Life in the monastery was dying. He went to his friend and wept. His friend, the rabbi, comforted him and told him: "There is something you need to know, my brother. We have long known in the Jewish community that the Messiah is one of you."

"What?" exclaimed the abbot. "The Messiah is one of us? How can that be?"

But the rabbi insisted that it was so, and the abbot went back to his monastery wondering and praying, comforted and excited.

Once back in the monastery, walking down the halls and in the courtyard, he would pass a monk and wonder if he was the one. Sitting in chapel, praying, he would hear a voice and look intently at a face and wonder if he was the one. And he began to treat all of his brothers with respect, with kindness and awe, with reverence. Soon it became quite noticeable.

One of the other brothers came to him and asked him what had happened. After some coaxing, the abbot told the brother what the rabbi had said. Soon the other monk was looking at his brothers differently and wondering.

Word spread through the monastery quickly: the Messiah is one of us. Soon the whole monastery was full of life, worship, kindness, and grace. The prayer life was rich and passionate, devoted, and the psalms and liturgy and services were alive and vibrant. Soon the surrounding villagers were coming to the services and listening and watching intently, and there were many who wished to join the community.

After their novitiate, when they took their vows, they were told the mystery, the truth that their life was based upon, the source of their strength and life together: the Messiah is one of us. The monastery grew and expanded into house after house, and all the monks grew in wisdom, age, and grace before the others and the eyes of God. And they say still, if you stumble across this place, where there is life and hope and kindness and graciousness, that the secret is the same: The Messiah is one of us.

With thanks to Sr. Doreen SSJD

If we want a healthy, loving community, we must treat one another as though the Messiah is one of us. As we know, at times this is not easy—especially if we cling to egoic consciousness.

Will the church as it is now collapse? Probably not in the near future, but it does face profound change as consciousness evolves and numbers decline. A new church is emerging, and how exciting is that!

A group of us were on our way home from a Contemplative Society retreat held on an island off Vancouver Island. We had a long wait for the ferry that would take us home, so someone suggested the retreat members form a circle on a patch of grass above the beach and the ferry dock. Each of us spontaneously took turns leading a chant. There was little organization; it just happened. Through the chanting and the silence, we literally carried the essence of the retreat out into the world.

Maybe the future church will look like this: more of a oneness with the world, more spontaneous, less organization, and all will be leaders and all followers. Maybe we are all meant to be priest-like crucibles of spiritual wisdom, as well as humble brothers and sisters—the non-dual incarnate. Jesus was like this. Other religions are probably going through similar profound changes. I am sure something wonderful will emerge.

Generosity and the Non-Dual

> Generosity is the most natural outward expression of an inner attitude of compassion and loving-kindness.
>
> Dalai Lama

> Across the world, across the street,
> the victims of injustice cry
> for shelter and for bread to eat,
> and never live until they die.
>
> Fred Pratt Green,
> "The Church of Christ in Every Age"

> Earth provides enough for everyone's need, but not for everyone's greed.
>
> Gandhi

> How does God's love abide in anyone who has the world's goods and sees a brother or sister in need and yet refuses help?
>
> 1 John 3:17

> We are all in this world together, and the only test of our character that matters is how we look after the least fortunate among us. How we look after

each other, not how we look after ourselves. That's all that really matters I think.

Tommy Douglas

The greatest story of generosity I can think of occurs in the Gospel of Mark 12:41–44, traditionally known as "the widow's mite." I know I could not give my last penny to charity, yet this destitute widow's faith is such that she does so. Amazing!

I find it disturbing that extremely wealthy people are praised and celebrated. There is only one thing we need to know about wealth—it is to be shared. Engineers Without Borders wrote: "In 2017, billionaires around the world increased their wealth by $762 billion—an amount that could have ended extreme global poverty seven times over!" I struggle to understand billionaires and I fail to understand a system which lets this happen. If the wealthy were truly generous they would no longer be wealthy, but then they would lose their "power and fame". Until these illusions are overcome, it is impossible to become compassion absolute. On rare occasions one hears of extremely wealthy people, like Warren Buffet, who say they will give away all their wealth. This is to be applauded of course, but it seems few wealthy people do this, and several years after this statement, Mr. Buffet is still an extremely wealthy man. Also, their largesse certainly helps people, but does it change the system that created the great disparity between people in the first place? I fear this gross and sickening disparity will continue until our egos are healed, transcended, and we come to a place of unitive/non-dual vision. This transformation will give us the political will to make the changes that are needed to make a more equal world.

I believe the more wealth is evenly distributed, the better the economy will be, and the healthier the world. As the old saying goes, "The better we all do—the better we all do."

I would be very happy to see a guaranteed income for everyone so that all were brought above the poverty line. People have said we can't afford such a system, but I believe in the old adage "Where there is a will there is a way." We must demand of ourselves and governments that we house the homeless and feed the hungry. Sadly, we do not demand anything of the sort. I heard it said years ago that the sign of good government is the absence of soup kitchens. We are far from that now.

Homelessness in a comparatively advanced country seems unnecessary. The fact that it is such a chronic problem tells us that we do not have the tender hearts we think we do, and have not done the spiritual work to create the will so that every person who wants a home will have one. Finland is working to eliminate homelessness, and the number of people who are living on the streets there has dropped by 35 percent between 2010 and 2018. The solution was "painfully simple and blindingly obvious: give homes to homeless people."[85] The political will is there, the spiritual work has been done. Other countries need to take note.

I am inspired by Anne Frank's words about generosity:

> We are all born alike. Everyone breathes the same air, a great many people believe in the same God. Everyone is born the same, everyone has to die, and nothing remains of their worldly glory. Riches, power, and fame last only a few years! Why do people cling so desperately to these transitory things?
>
> Why can't people who have more than they need for themselves give that surplus to their fellow citizens? Why should some people have such a hard time during their few years on this earth?
>
> Give of yourself; give as much as you can! And you can always, always give something, even if it is only kindness. Give and you shall receive, much more than you would have thought possible. Give, give again and again, don't lose courage, keep it up and go on giving!

There is plenty of room for everyone in the world, enough money, riches, and beauty for all to share. God has made enough for everyone. Let us begin then by sharing it fairly.

Many cultures have a word for this fair sharing. In South Africa, for instance, they call it *Ubuntu*.

Writing about generosity and abundant giving reminds me of a simple song I learned when I taught Sunday School. The song tells us all we really need to know.

Love is something if you give it away, give it away, give it away,
Love is something if you give it away, you end up having more.
It's just like a magic penny, hold it tight and you won't have any,
Lend it, spend it, and you'll have so many they'll roll all over the floor.
Oh love is something if you give it away, give it away, give it away,
Love is something if you give it away, you end up having more.

This beautiful prayer about community, generosity, and justice is a natural bridge to the next section.

Loving God,
Give bread to those who are hungry.
Give hunger for justice to those who have bread.[86]

Transcendent Justice

Focusing on something gives energy to it. A change from focusing on the excessive hoarding of money to focusing on generosity is an example of a paradigm shift of consciousness. So too is a move from punitive justice to restorative justice.

These kinds of shifts will bring dramatic change for the better to our world.

The three questions punitive justice asks are: What was the crime? Who did it? How can we punish them?

Restorative justice asks: Who was hurt? What do they need? How can we help?

The focus of restorative justice shifts the paradigm to healing the "disease" around the crime. The spiritual journey can take us beyond restorative justice to transcended justice, yet another shift in consciousness and paradigm.

I know of no better example of transcended justice than Thomas Keating's story of the woman whose son was murdered, an amazing story of inner work and the kingdom of God acting "in concert." As a result, a beautiful "sound" emerges from utterly terrible suffering and grief. A woman's only son, just finishing college with the promise of a brilliant future, was shot to death on the street by a sociopath. With agonizing grief in her heart and many harrowing questions in her mind, the mother decided to write and tell her son's murderer that she forgave him.

> For a year she received no response. Finally a very matter-of-fact letter came, acknowledging her letter but without the least sign of remorse. She wrote back asking if he would be willing to see her. Again a wait of about a year. Finally a note came saying yes. She drove the long distance to the prison, and accompanied by the social worker assigned to his case, she met the murderer of her son. He spent most of the time describing, absolutely deadpan, the horrendous childhood he had suffered. He was an unwanted child, continually subjected to physical abuse in the extreme. As a consequence, he had become totally antisocial and narcissistic. At one point in the conversation, he confessed, "You

cannot imagine the immense joy I felt when I stood over your son and realized that I had killed him!" It was his moment of ultimate power. For the first time the sense of self-worth that had been systematically crushed by his whole previous life experience flooded over him to the point of ecstatic triumph.

The mother stood her ground. Her forgiveness was unshaken, and she reaffirmed it to him. The social worker was flabbergasted by the spirit of this woman who could calmly forgive the one who had caused her the greatest pain of her life. The social worker wrote to her sometime later saying, "This man has started to change. He shows a little more courtesy and consideration for the other inmates."

The woman felt moved to stay in contact with the prisoner. She offered to return. His immediate response was poignant: "Please don't come again. I'm afraid if you keep coming, I'll have to face the unbearable pain of my childhood." His antisocial behavior had enabled him to maintain absolute denial of a past that was too painful to face up to. But she did go back. At the end of the interview, she embraced him.

Thomas Keating says, "I do not know what the final outcome of this exchange will be. She is still writing, still visiting him, still feeling the pain of her great loss. In her last interview, she detected as she gave him a farewell hug, a tiny tear in the corner of his eye. In a very real sense, she has become his mother and he is becoming her son."[87] This is transformative justice. The prisoner's terrible memories of horrific abuse are being healed and transformed by unconditional love.

I have heard few other stories that speak so strongly and clearly about the kingdom of God and the healing of the universe. The mother of the murdered man has indeed become compassion absolute and an example of non-dual consciousness.

Peace

> If we have no peace, it is because we have forgotten
> that we belong to each other.

Mother Teresa

> Last night I had the strangest dream
> I'd ever had before
> I dreamed the world had all agreed
> To put an end to war

Ed McCurdy

My father was a volunteer for the Canadian Army in World War II. He would occasionally tell us, his family, stories of the war, usually with happy or humorous endings, although he much preferred to tell stories from the depression years of the 1930s. Only on one or two occasions did he recount bad things that happened during his war years. When my sister asked him point blank what it felt like to kill someone, he said he would rather not talk about it.

A couple of months before he died I heard him say for the first and only time that "going to war was a mistake." I believe that by making that statement he was coming close to the spiritual world. A veil of illusion had been lifted.

One of the most difficult teachings to learn must be "love your enemies"; if it were easy, surely we would have world peace. We think that we love each other, but often we haven't got a clue. When I have been really angry with someone, I have found loving my enemy an almost impossible challenge. I admit I have to work on this, but exercising my letting go muscle in centering prayer helps a great deal. As Cynthia Bourgeault says, "Action flows better when it flows from nonviolence, that is, from that place of relaxed, inner opening."[88]

When people are asked what they want most for the world, the answer often is "world peace." Most would say that world peace was achievable. And why not? With God, all things are possible. When the world reaches a certain point in its spiritual maturity, true democracy and world peace will be there for us. As long as we believe in violence, we will always suffer, but when we *really* begin to believe in love, the suffering will start to ebb. I believe we are making strides. As I have passed my 60th year, there is more peace in the world than at any other time in my life.

By now I must sound like a broken record, because world peace will only be achieved by our inner work and our inner being. Instead of bracing our hearts toward others, we must soften and surrender our hearts to God.

I know from experience that this is easier said than done. I believe one of the most effective ways to bring peace into the world is to let go and heal the inner violence within us, the negative, critical thoughts that are often directed at ourselves as well as others. These kinds of thoughts send negativity and fear out into the world.

As I have discussed several times already, the small shift from egoic to spiritual consciousness creates miracles because it allows us to see the larger picture, and also allows us to unite with other realms, such as the communion of saints, who are more than willing and able to help us.

I firmly believe in the vision expounded in the books of Isaiah and Micah (how can one not?): "They shall beat their swords into ploughshares and their spears into pruning hooks; nation shall not lift sword against nation, neither shall they learn war anymore" (Isaiah 2:4 and Micah 4:3). This vision is echoed in Christian hymns, such as "O God of Every Nation"—

> Keep bright in us the vision of days when war shall cease,
> when hatred and division give way to love and peace.

Let us keep the vision bright! Rejoice and be excited because the vision is coming into being. Research shows that over the last few centuries death from war has greatly decreased, even though this decrease seems tragically and painfully slow. As Mark Kurlansky wrote in his book about nonviolence, "But there is in Tao, as in Hinduism, the notion that human beings evolve and the more highly evolved human beings do not need physical violence."[89] (And very highly evolved human beings have no need of any kind of violence.) We may need only a small shift of heart and mind for the change to world peace to evolve rapidly. To bring it into being with the least amount of suffering, we must continually say yes to God and the inner journey.

The invasion of Iraq in 2003 was an excellent test of our collective spiritual muscles. Millions of people around the world protested the invasion of Iraq by the United States and a small number of coalition countries. There was enough spiritual oomph to delay the war but not stop it. Soon, I hope, we will have enough inner strength to stop any war we wish. Sadly, we can still be talked into war, but the time is coming in our collective spiritual journey when, in every circumstance, we will have the consciousness to say no to the evils of war. I see the day coming, in the not-too-distant future I hope, when there will be a world without armed forces. It is not soldiers but those who know how to love their enemies who give us our freedom.

There are nations that say, "We must use violence or our country will cease to exist." I say, "Rubbish!" If you have to use violence, should your country exist? If we love one another, we will always exist and we will not feel threatened. We can justify every violent thought or action and say how right we are, but the inner spiritual journey is not about justification but about transformation.

It has taken me many years to come to the conclusion that violence is always wrong, and the proof or fruit of this is that violence always leads to unforeseen suffering. If you have to use force to control a situation, you are in severe spiritual failure—and Christians who are violent against another have broken their baptismal vows. When we learn true compassion, we win every battle without having to be violent! If you ever have a non-dual mystical experience then war is no longer an option.

A great benefit of inner work is the ability to stop and reflect that we are in spiritual failure as soon as we notice we are doing, saying, or thinking anything violent, and then a willingness to ask for help to find another way. As in all things, this works on a personal level as well as a global level.

I wish to share the small but telling stories of two peacemakers. The first person will forever remain anonymous to me in this life, but the one action I saw her do many years ago impressed me so much that I will never forget it. It took place at a meeting to debate nuclear armament. Both pro- and anti-nuclear advocates were present. As you can imagine, there was a lot of acrimony flying around. A middle-aged woman on the pro-nuclear-weapon side suddenly got up and announced in a loud voice that she was leaving the meeting. A younger woman, in genuine tenderness and concern, ignored the negative atmosphere around her, and reached out to the middle-aged woman, and said, "Oh, don't go." The older woman said, "I *am* going." Although the older woman tried to maintain her huffy, righteous indignation, you could sense it had been shattered by the other woman's genuine tenderness. It was a small act but had great impact. The younger woman was practising a form of "moral jujitsu": "The attacker expects resistance, and when there is none he loses his 'moral balance.'"[90]

The second peacemaker was a member of the first prayer group I joined and also one of the founders of the Raging Grannies. For a time in the 1980s and 1990s, a small group of people held a peace vigil for an hour every Wednesday on a corner in downtown Victoria. Most people would ignore us, some would agree with our stance, and others were downright hostile to us. Doran was superb at engaging hostile people. She would ask them, "What do you think?" Gradually, as she communicated in a calm way, their hostility would dissipate and they would often end up having a pleasant conversation.

People may say, "That is all very nice, but if you were threatened with immediate violence to yourself or a loved one, you would do anything, violence included, to end the situation." It is true; I don't know how I would act as I have never been in that position. However, I know of two people in such situations who by their inner presence, and most certainly with help from other realms, were able to defuse a dangerous situation. As Cynthia Bourgeault says, "Terrorism only has a hook when we are afraid to die." It all seems to come back to self-emptying. Ridding the world of war and armaments has many positive and far-reaching effects. For one thing, if we really care about those who are hungry and those who are homeless, we will give up war because we will realize that, through the enormous cost of armaments and paid armies, we are robbing them. World War II military leader Dwight D. Eisenhower woke up to this and wrote, "Every gun that is made, every warship launched, every rocket fired, signifies in the final sense a theft from those who are hungry and are not fed, those who are cold and not clothed." When we see the trillions of dollars spent around the world on armaments and war, we must wake up and realize that we have been sleepwalking in evil.

Mark Kurlansky's *Nonviolence: Twenty-five Lessons from the History of a Dangerous Idea* is an insightful history of violence and peace through the ages. He writes that Christians of the first couple of centuries were "uncompromisingly dedicated to pacifism . . . Then came the triumph of Christianity, a calamity from which the Church has never recovered . . . One of history's greatest lessons is that once the state embraces a religion, the nature of that religion changes radically. It loses its nonviolent component and becomes a force for war rather than peace."[91]

Here are some more thoughts on violence and nonviolence from his book:

> Marching against the Korean War in 1951, [Bayard Rustin] was attacked with a stick by an angry spectator. Rustin handed him a second stick and asked him if he wanted to use both. The attacker threw both sticks down.

> The practice of violence changes the world, but the most probable change is a more violent world.
>
> Hannah Arendt

> Adam Michnik, writing from [a Polish] prison in 1985, gave several arguments in favor of nonviolence. Michnik, who grew up in the repressive society created by the Russian Revolution, wrote: "Taught by history, we suspect that by using force to storm the existing Bastilles we shall unwittingly build new ones." He said, "In our reasoning, pragmatism is inseparably intertwined with idealism." And this approach may be characteristic of all successful nonviolent activists. It is what perplexed Orwell about Gandhi. Michnik did not believe violence was a viable option for his cause. As he put it simply: "We have no guns."

My prayer is that a non-dual way of seeing becomes deeply rooted in all of us. At that point, a nonviolent solution becomes the only possible course of action.

> Love one another as I have loved you.
>
> Jesus of Nazareth

AND NOW FOR A BIT OF ESCHATOLOGY . . .

Another world is not only possible, she is on her way. On a quiet day I can hear her breathing.

Arundhati Roy

My heart shall sing of the day you bring,
Let the fires of your justice burn,
Wipe away all tears,
For the dawn draws near
And the world is about to turn.

"The Canticle of the Turning"

Since Love is lord of heaven and earth,
How can I keep from singing?

"My Life Flows On in Endless Song"

L ike Arundhati Roy, I believe we can sense the kingdom of God, a far better world, but only if we are attentive to silence. If we are attentive to silence and the inner world, we shall indeed see the world turn. Therefore, if we want world peace, we must say yes to our inner (spiritual) work; if we want a disease-free world, we must say yes to our inner work; if we want less suffering, we must say yes to our inner work. Self-emptying, of which Jesus is a supreme example, is at the heart of inner work, but for many of us this is a difficult thing to come to.

I believe we make a mistake when we say "I could never be like Jesus." The same spiritual nature manifested in such masters as Jesus Christ and the Buddha is accessible to each of us.

We can be distracted by, or worry about, fundamentalism, but the really deep stuff is doing the great work. The great work is healing the world from the inside out. Fundamentalism, which can result in extreme behaviour, is a certain stage, but when we go deeper or to a higher stage, the superficiality of fundamentalism dissipates and we begin to see ourselves and the world turn. It is the deep things that last, not the superficial.

> Life progresses; evolution advances on all levels. The wider and more complete the spread of tolerance, understanding, forgiveness, the stronger and more potent will be the Rays of spiritual advancement which will enhance the evolution of man. The greater the spread of spiritual knowledge, the more speedy will be the enlightenment and upliftment of humans into harmony and peace.[92]

I sense this statement has a lot of truth in it. In some circles it is called the breakthrough of the spirit, and it brings incredible hope for a better world for all life on Earth. It also opens us not only to the realms of pure love and light but to darker, unpurified realms as well. So there are dangers. To avoid the dangers we must be deeply rooted in love.

I strongly sense that the spiritual world is being revealed more and more in this world. Sometimes we sense the excitement. Spiritual evolution may be slowed or suffer setbacks but it cannot be stopped. The communion of saints never sleeps. Their work is so subtle and gentle (but persistent!) that unless we are attuned to this subtle world, we can find ourselves flat on the floor with the rug pulled from under us. We are literally floored and bewildered by where a new reality has come from. If we are awake, however, we can see it coming. Even better, if we have surrendered to the divine love, we can help give birth to the new reality.

Thomas Merton once took a photo that he called "the only known photo of God." It was a picture of a giant hook. God/ love is the great attractor in the universe. For a moment let us think that love might be most powerfully reflected in the physical world as gravity. On a small scale its effects are barely sensed but very much present. On a large scale it seems to be responsible for the geography (for want of a better word) of the space/time realm. Current models suggest gravity was the first force to break from the unified oneness of the Big Bang.

> Something big is coming. It's still secret, but arriving everywhere . . . The atmosphere is charged with longing and searching. Then the sound of prayer drifts across the dawn. It's Muslim, Jew, and Christian all mingled . . .
>
> Rumi

So Rumi wrote in the thirteenth century. "It" has been coming a long time.

The medieval mystic Joachim of Fiore believed history to be divided into bi-millennial units, with seven millennia altogether. In his outline of history, from the beginning of time (as it seemed to those in the medieval times) to the birth of Christ, the primary emphasis was on God the Father. From the coming of Christ to 2000 CE, the primary emphasis was on God the Son. From 2000 CE to 4000 CE, the primary emphasis in worship and in human affairs will be on God the Spirit. The era from 4000 to 5000 CE will be the consummate and glorious union of all three parts of the Godhead within space/ time.[93] Who knows if this is a correct model. But I believe in any case that the Earth is in for some marvellous and exciting times—"far more than all we can ask or imagine," as St. Paul has written (Ephesians 3:20).

Some scientists believe that the universe will eventually end as nothing but cold dark matter, all energy expended. Some see this as futility—but it will not be! Perhaps every subatomic particle will have been transformed and become love and wisdom.

This is reiterated by the fourteenth-century Christian mystic Hadewijch of Antwerp—"And so the dark river of history moves on, creeping ever closer to the place of its beginning, the moment of its nativity . . . And as the river moves be sure—no work of love is ever lost."

> God coming from God
> Light streaming from Light,
> inaccessible, incomprehensible to all,
> yet open to the human heart forever.
> Glory upon glory
> Radiance filling radiance,
> light streaming to us and drawing us (home) back
> again.
>
> For you cast us like sunlight upon the earth,
> And your light, passing through our bodies
> as if it were an open window to our Source,
> returns, purified, to You
>
> Rumi

In the words of the Jesuit priest Anthony de Mello: "Extend your arms in welcome to the future! The best is yet to come!" I believe the best is indeed yet to come. Let us go forward in the joy of hope and love!

BOOKS FOR FURTHER READING AND REFLECTION

Mary-Wynne Ashford with Guy Dauncey, *Enough Blood Shed* (Gabriola Island, BC: New Society Publishers, 2006). This book bursts with ideas and examples of how to bring peace into the world.

Cynthia Bourgeault, *Centering Prayer and Inner Awakening* (Cambridge, MA: Cowley Publications, 2004). Both this book and the next are essential reading if you practise, or even just want to know about, centering prayer. They are extremely comprehensive books on the subject.

Cynthia Bourgeault, *The Heart of Centering Prayer: Nondual Christianity in Theory and Practice* (Boulder, CO: Shambhala, 2016). This book has developed from Cynthia's thirty-plus years of practising and teaching centering prayer. It wonderfully connects centering prayer with the leading-edge consciousness of nonduality.

Cynthia Bourgeault, *The Wisdom Way of Knowing: Reclaiming an Ancient Tradition to Awaken the Heart* (San Francisco: Jossey-Bass Publishers, 2003). This gem of a book is full of stories of inner insight. I quote from it often in *Pool of Wisdom*.

Maggie Callanan and Patricia Kelley, *Final Gifts: Understanding the Special Awareness, Needs and Communications of the Dying* (New York: Simon & Schuster, 2012). This is the best book I've read about the hospice movement, care of the dying, and the experiences of the dying.

Anthony de Mello, *Wellsprings: A Book of Spiritual Exercises* (Doubleday, 1984). A collection of lovely spiritual meditations.

Micheal Finkel, *The Stranger in the Woods: The Extraordinary Story of the Last True Hermit* (New York: Alfred A. Knopf, 2017). For those interested in solitude, I strongly recommend Chapter 22 of this book, which is packed with wisdom about solitude from many sources.

Helen Greaves, *Testimony of Light* (London: Rider, 2005). Helen Greaves and Frances Banks are mystical seekers and fellow members of the Churches' Fellowship for Psychical and Spiritual Studies. After Frances physically dies, Helen, who has mediumistic and telepathic abilities, relates Frances's story of her new life in the spiritual world. One of my favourite books by a medium.

Helen Greaves, *The Wheel of Eternity* (London: Neville Spearman Ltd., 1974). From the first time I read this book, I found it fascinating, though others find it very unsettling. It is the factual story of a spiritual medium, Helen Greaves, who becomes part of a story that unfolds in the eternal. With help from advanced beings in the spiritual realm and Helen in the physical realm, beings who have physically died come to be healed and are able to evolve spiritually.

Edward Hayes, *Prayers for a Planetary Pilgrim* (Leavenworth, KS: Forest of Peace Publishing, 1996). I have used the beautiful prayers and meditations in this book many times. There is an apt prayer for any occasion and every season, and prayers for many world faiths.

Kabir Edmund Helminski, *Living Presence: A Sufi Way to Mindfulness and the Essential Self* (New York: Tarcher/Putnam, 1992). This is the best book I know for learning about inner work. Many small groups within the Contemplative Society and other contemplative groups have used this book. The group I was in studied this remarkable book on inner work for four years. Its practical companion by Lynn Bauman is *Living the Presence: A Manual for Contemplative Christian Practice* (Telephone, TX: Praxis, 1996).

Thomas Keating, *The Kingdom of God is Like . . .* (New York: Crossroad Publishing, 1993). This book offers reflections on the parables of the Gospels and some profound stories from contemporary life—see the story in the section "Justice Transcended."

Thomas Keating, *Open Mind, Open Heart* (New York: Continuum Publishing, 1997). A primer on centering prayer by one of the founders of the practice.

Mark Kurlansky, *Nonviolence: Twenty-five Lessons from the History of a Dangerous Idea* (New York: Random House, 2006). This is an absolute must read for those integrating nonviolence into their lives. This book makes your heart burn.

Daniel Ladinsky, *Love Poems from God: Twelve Sacred Voices from the East and West* (New York: Penguin Compass, 2002). This is a beautiful book full of love and wisdom. The short readings are perfect for leading into silent meditation.

Robert Lanza and Bob Berman, *Beyond Biocentrism: Rethinking Time, Space, Consciousness, and the Illusion of Death* (Dallas, TX: BenBella Books, 2016). An excellent book that scientists need to take more note of. I believe biocentrism has the ability to bring science and religion/spirituality into harmony.

Jacques Lusseyran, *And There Was Light,* 3rd ed. (Novato, CA: New World Library, 2014). This is an excellent autobiography by a blind hero of the French Resistance. An amazing read, especially for those interested in spiritual work. Lusseyran writes with extraordinary perception about the inner world. Even in the horrors of Buchenwald he could find light and joy. See pages 9, 10, and 185. "The first of these is that joy does not come from outside, for whatever happens to us it is within. The second truth is that light does not come to us from without. Light is in us, even if we have no eyes" (page 244).

Gunilla Norris, *Inviting Silence: Universal Principles of Meditation* (Katonah, NY: Blue Bridge Books, 2004). In this beautiful little book, Gunilla Norris displays profound knowledge of silence and meditation. An excellent source book for Quiet Days or meditation times.

Joyce Rupp, *Praying Our Goodbyes* (Notre Dame, IN: Ave Maria Press, 1988). I have found Rupp's books to be extremely helpful. I feel very privileged to have met this beautiful and deeply spiritual person.

Valentin Tomberg, *Meditations on the Tarot* (New York: Penguin Putnam, 2002). This is considered one of the best books ever written on Christian mysticism. You must be a serious student of Christian mysticism because it is quite the tome and requires some perseverance to get through. It is well worth it however, as Tomberg plumbs the depths.

Jim B. Tucker, *Return to Life: Extraordinary Cases of Children Who Remember Past Lives* (New York: St. Martin's Press, 2013). The stories of children who remember their past lives are very compelling, but it is Chapters 8 and 9, which deal with consciousness, that blow my mind all the way down to my heart! In these two chapters Dr. Tucker addresses consciousness from the point of view of quantum mechanics. He writes about consciousness and quantum mechanics with such clarity and readability it is very profound and enlightening.

Jurgen Ziewe, *Vistas of Infinity: How to Enjoy Life When You Are Dead* (Self-published through Lightning Source UK Ltd., 2015). Through deep meditation and lucid dreaming, Jurgen Ziewe has had out-of-body experiences that allow him to visit non-local states of consciousness and post-life territories in full waking awareness. I found this book very enlightening, and it confirmed some thoughts I have had for some time about life in the spirit, such as entanglement and reincarnation. Jurgen's experiences get the wheels turning in my mind.

Tao De Ching Parts of this remind me of the Gospel of Thomas.

Bhagavad Gita

OTHER RESOURCES

For those interested in the contemplative path, practices, events, and retreats, the Contemplative Society has a wonderful website: www.contemplative.org There are several similar organizations on the web: Center for Action and Contemplation (https://cac.org/), Northeast Wisdom (https://northeastwisdom.org/), Wisdom School Southwest, and Wisdom Way of Knowing (https://wisdomwayofknowing.org/), are a few in the Christian faith.

The Wisdom School Community Facebook page has some marvellous and deeply moving offerings from many different people.

If you have questions for me, I would be happy to answer them and discuss the material in this book. Please contact me at mcsbook59@gmail.com

Happy seeking, asking, and knocking!

ENDNOTES

1   Quoted in Rita F. Snowden, The Time of Our Lives (Nashville, TN: Abingdon Press, 1966), p. 65.

2   If you are interested, please visit the Contemplative Society's website at www.contemplative.org and click on the contemplative practices tab.

3   It is now considered that there are more than five major religions. I can think of at least seven.

4   Paulo Coelho, Brida (New York: Harper Collins, 2008), p. 47.

5   From a retreat with Rev. Matthew Wright, "Opening to the Eye of the Heart," March 17–22, 2017.

6   Valentin Tomberg, Meditations on the Tarot (New York: Penguin Putnam, 2002), p. 511. In this paragraph on page 511, and on the following page or two, Tomberg writes interestingly about the "surface world," the "depth world," and the "guardian of the threshold."

7   John Polkinghorne, Science and the Trinity: The Christian Encounter with Reality (New Haven, CT: Yale University Press, 2004), p. 72.

8   Annie Dillard, Pilgrim at Tinker Creek (New York: Harper's Magazine Press, 1974), p. 216.

9   Kabir Edmund Helminski, Living Presence: A Sufi Way to Mindfulness and the Essential Self (New York: Penguin Putnam, 1992), p. 157.

10 Henri Nouwen, The Only Necessary Thing (New York: The Crossroad Publishing Company, 1999), p. 147.

11 I am very grateful to Father Thomas Keating for bringing this Sufi story to my attention.

12 This is also echoed in St. Augustine's Confessions: "Late Have I loved you, Beauty so ancient and so new! Lo, you were within, but I was outside, seeking there for you."

13 Quoted by Cynthia Bourgeault in Centering Prayer and Inner Awakening (Cambridge, MA: Cowley Publications, 2004), p. 107.

14 Une grande amitie: Correspondance 1926–1972, Julien Green—Jacques Maritain (Paris: Gallimard, 1982), p. 282.

15 As described by Phyllis Tickle in The Great Emergence: How Christianity Is Changing and Why (Grand Rapids, MI: Baker Books, 2008), p. 88.

16 A life of pain and poverty is more or less true. No person should have to endure such pain and I have never made an income over the poverty level. However, I have been fortunate and have never been homeless.

17 Cynthia Bourgeault, Wisdom Way of Knowing (San Francisco: Jossey-Bass Publishers, 2003), p. 25.

18 If ICA69 does turn out to be the culprit for Sjogren syndrome, it would be misleading to call it an autoimmune disease. It would be better to call it an autoallergy disease. If you want to know more about this research Google: ICA69 primary Sjogren syndrome

19 I have set up an ICA69 Research Fund. To help with this or donate to this research project please contact me through this email: mcsbook59@gmail.com.

20 Used with the kind permission of Joyce Rupp.

21 Quoted in Jim B. Tucker, Return to Life: Extraordinary Cases of Children Who Remember Past Lives (New York: St. Martin's Press, 2013), p. 168.

22 Gebser wouldn't like my using the words "evolution" or "progression" of consciousness. I think "unfolding" would be more acceptable to him. This is why I have named this chapter The Unfolding of Consciousness. See the Wikipedia article on Gebser.

23 "Omega point" was coined by Pierre Teilhard de Chardin S.J. (1881–1955).

24 Ken Wilber, Integral Spirituality (Boston: Integral Books, 2006), pp. 258, 259.

25 Rick Groleau, "Imagining Other Dimensions," Nova Website, July 2003, http://www.pbs.org/wgbh/nova/physics/imagining-other-dimensions.html.

26 This paradigm shift pattern is taken from Cynthia Bourgeault's "Cloud of Unknowing" retreat, September 27, 2002.

27 Maurice Nicoll, Psychological Commentaries on the Teaching of Gurdjieff and Ouspensky, vol. 5 (Boulder, CO: Shambhala, 1984), p. 543.

28 Tomberg, Meditations on the Tarot, p. 91.

29 Quoted in Netanel Miles-Yepez, ed., The Common Heart: An Experience of Interreligious Dialogue (Brooklyn, NY: Lantern Books, 2006), p. 84.

30 Gerald May, Will and Spirit (New York: HarperCollins Publishers, 1987), p. 238.

31 Ibid, p. 239.

32 Malcolm Gladwell, Outliers: The Story of Success (New York: Little, Brown and Company, 2008), pp. 283–84.

33 John Welwood, Toward a Psychology of Awakening (Boston: Shambhala Publishing, 2000), p. 170.

34 Greg Mortenson and David Oliver Relin, Three Cups of Tea: One Man's Mission to Promote Peace . . . One School at a Time (New York: Penguin Books, 2006), pp. 152–53. Sadly, it has come to light that some of the stories in Three Cups of Tea may be fabrications. Even if this story is a fabrication, it is still a wonderful example of seeing the larger picture.

35 Quoted in Vikram Seth, A Suitable Boy (Boston: Little, Brown and Company, 1993.), p. 550.

36 In Matthew Fox, Meditations with Meister Eckhart (Rochester, VT: Bear and Company, 1983), p. 99.

37 Tomberg, Meditations on the Tarot, p. 11.

38 Kathy Galloway, ed., The Pattern of Our Days: Worship in the Celtic Tradition from the Iona Community (Mahwah, NJ: Paulist Press, 1996), pp. 96–97.

39 Richard Wagamese, Medicine Walk (Toronto: McClelland and Stewart, 2014), p. 33.

40 This is a quote from one of Cynthia Bourgeault's spiritual teachers, Fr. Rafe Robbin OSB.

41 This group included Thomas Keating, Basil Pennington, and William Menninger.

42 Correspondence via e-mail from Cynthia Bourgeault, April 26, 2011.

43 Christopher Page, Christ Wisdom (Toronto: Dundurn Press, 2004), p. 46.

44 Adyashanti, Jesus: Unifying Human and Divine, Retreat, December 2014, at Asilomar State Park Conference Centre, Pacific Grove, CA.

45 Correspondence via e-mail from Cynthia Bourgeault, April 26, 2011.

46 Quoted in Perry Garfinkel, Buddha or Bust: In Search of Truth, Meaning, Happiness, and the Man Who Found Them All (New York: Three Rivers Press, 2006), p. 4.

47 Lynn Bauman. Living the Presence: A Manual for Contemplative Christian Practice. (Telephone, TX: Praxis, 1996), p. 11.

48 Kabir Edmund Helminski, Living Presence: A Sufi Way to Mindfulness and the Essential Self (New York: Penguin Putnam, 1992), p. 157.

49 Thomas Keating, Invitation to Love: The Way of Christian Contemplation (New York: The Continuum Publishing Company, 1995.), p. 3.

50 From a talk given by Selinde Krayenhoff on Centering Prayer.

51 Ibid.

52 From a Prayer after Communion from the Book of Alternative Services of Anglican Church of Canada, p. 214, but ultimately from St. Paul and Ephesians 3:20.

53 Bourgeault, Centering Prayer and Inner Awakening, p. 77.

54 Arthur Guirdham, The Nature of Healing (London: George Allen and Unwin, 1964), p. 154. This quote can also be found in Rev. Angus Haddow, "The Energy of Many Names," The Christian Parapsychologist. 15, no. 2 (June 2002): pp. 39–40.

55 Eileen Curteis SSA, Reiki: A Spiritual Doorway to Natural Healing (Victoria, BC: Trafford Publishing, 2004), p. 61.

56 Ibid., p. 66.

57   Ibid., p. 8.
58   Jurgen Ziewe, Vistas of Infinity: How to Enjoy Life When You Are
     Dead (Milton Keynes, UK: Lightning Source, UK Ltd., 2015) p. 86.
59   Keely was a board member of the Contemplative Society. She
     was in her 20s when she wrote this statement in a Contemplative
     Society newsletter.
60   Timothy Freke, The Wisdom of the Christian Mystics. (Boston,
     MA: Journey Editions, 1998), p. 8.
61   Ibid.
62   Thomas Merton, Conjectures of a Guilty Bystander, p. 56.
63   Cited in Robert Lanza and Bob Berman, Beyond Biocentrism:
     Rethinking Time, Space, Consciousness, and the Illusion of
     Death (Dallas, TX: BenBella Books, 2016), p. 112.
64   Bourgeault, Wisdom Way of Knowing, p. 52.
65   Lanza and Berman, Beyond Biocentrism, p. 74
66   Frances Mayes, Bella Tuscany (New York: Broadway Books,
     1999), p. 152.
67   People have reported becoming more sensitive telepathically and
     psychically after experiencing blows to the right side of the head.
68   Thanks to Herbert O'Driscoll for bringing Machado's poem
     to my attention. "Last Night" is from Times Alone—Selected
     Poems of Antonio Machado, trans. Robert Bly (Middletown,
     CT: Wesleyan University Press, 1983), p. 43.
69   Bourgeault, Wisdom Way of Knowing, p. 74.
70   Gail Godwin, Heart: A Personal Journey Through Its Myths
     and Meanings (New York: William Morrow Publishers, 2001),
     pp. 5–6.
71   Ziewe, Vistas of Infinity, p. 22.
72   Quoted in Humphrey Carpenter, The Inklings: C.S. Lewis,
     J.R.R. Tolkien, Charles Williams and Their Friends (Boston:
     Houghton Mifflin, 1978), p. 204.
73   Henri Nouwen, Life of the Beloved: Spiritual Living in a Secular
     World (New York: Crossroad Publishing, 1992), p. 96.
74   These are all taken from Jan Karon, Patches of Godlight: Father
     Tim's Favorite Quotes (New York: Putnam, 2001).
75   Polkinghorne, Science and the Trinity, p. 160.
76   Ibid., p. 159.

77 Helen Greaves, *The Wheel of Eternity* (London: Neville Spearman, 1974) pp. 59 and 126.

78 Jurgen Ziewe, Vistas of Infinity, p. 95.

79 Nouwen, Life of the Beloved, p. 110.

80 "Remember, we perceive only a limited range of electromagnetic wavelengths and only feel objects because our electrical fields are encountering theirs." Lanza and Berman, Beyond Biocentrism, p. 82.

81 Quote from Lynn Bauman's afternoon talk on May 19, 2001, at "Mining More Deeply Our Wisdom Tradition," Retreat Intensive with Lynn Bauman and Cynthia Bourgeault, May 18–20, 2001.

82 Quotes from Gene Miller's article in Focus Magazine, February 2007, p. 46.

83 Bourgeault, Wisdom Way of Knowing, p. 26.

84 Nathan Ball, L'Arche Foundation newsletter, April 8, 2011.

85 Harry Quilter-Pinner, "Finland Has Found the Answer to Homelessness. It Couldn't Be Simpler," The Guardian, April 12, 2018, https://www.theguardian.com/commentisfree/2018/apr/12/finland-homelessness-rough-sleepers-britain

86 A South African table grace from Sabina Alkire and Edmund Newell, What Can One Person Do? Faith to Heal a Broken World (New York: Church Publishing, 2005), p. 41.

87 Thomas Keating, The Kingdom of God Is Like . . . (New York: Crossroad Publishing, 1993), pp. 44–45.

88 Bourgeault, Wisdom Way of Knowing, p. 75.

89 Mark Kurlansky, Nonviolence: Twenty-five Lessons from the History of a Dangerous Idea (New York: Random House, 2006), pp. 11–12.

90 Ibid., 153. Philosopher Richard Gregg developed the concept of moral jujitsu to explain how nonviolent actions work.

91 Ibid, pp. 21, 24–25.

92 Greaves, The Wheel of Eternity, p. 80.

93 Phyllis Tickle, The Great Emergence, pp. 164-65. Thanks to Rev. Carmen Simmonds for bringing this book to my attention.

INDEX

CPSIA information can be obtained
at www.ICGtesting.com
Printed in the USA
LVHW111716260720
661576LV00002B/309